CYPRUS

SELAS LTD

ISBN 9963 566 82 0

Cyprus

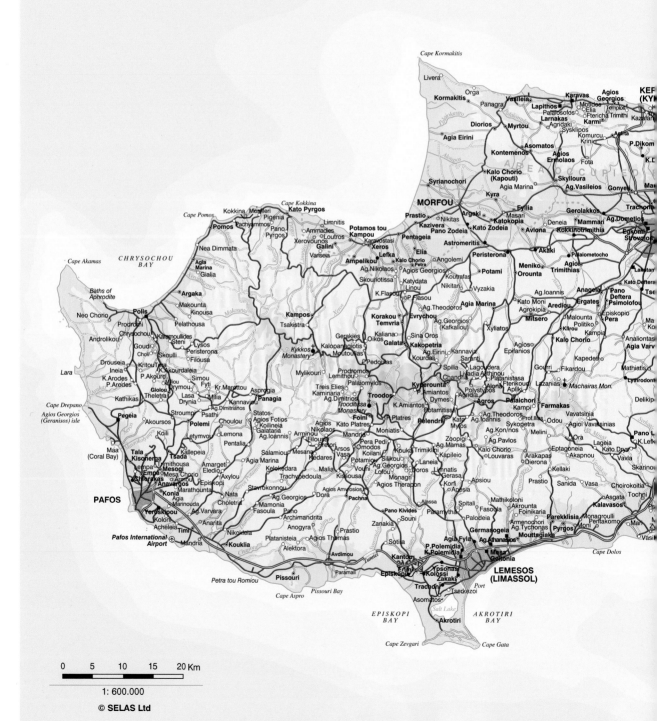

0   5   10   15   20 Km

1: 600.000

Cape Apostolos Andreas

Rizokarpaso

N

Cape Plakoti

Gialousa **Agia Trias**
Melanarga
Agios Koroveia **Galinoporni**
Andronikos Koilanemos
Lythragkomi Agios Symeon
Platanissos Vasili **Vathylakas**
Leonarisso Neta
Eptakomi **Koma tou Gialou**
Davlos **Komi Kebir** **Galateia**
Flamoudi Krideia Livadia
Agios Tavrou
Ovgoros Efstathios Vokolida
Akanthou Ardana Geroni **Patriki** **Agios**
Mandres **Avgolida** **Theodoros**
Ag.Andronikos Cape Elia
Agios **Kalograia** (Topou Köy) Gastria
Amvrosios Ag. Ag.Iakovos
Charkeia Nikolaos Artemi Ag.Ilias
(Chartzeia) Melounta Platani Monarga
Ag.Chariton Trypimeni Perivolia tou
Kornokipos Goufes Trikomou
Kalyvakia **Knodara** **Lapathos** **Trikomo**
Kythrea **Kiados** **Gypsou** Sygkrasis
Bey Köy Petra tou Digeni Psyllatos **Lefkonoiko** Ag. Georgios
Epicho Kourou Vitsada **Milia** Arnadi
Voni Monastiri **Spathariko**
Exo Metochi **Marathovounos** Genagra Pigi
Palaikythro **Peristerona** Maratha Aloda **Agios**
Angastina Mousoulita Santalaris **Limnia** **Sergios**
Mora Pyrga
OSIA **Askeia** **Prastio** **Stylloi**
SIA) **(Asseia)** Strongylos Gaidouras **Eakomi**
Afanteia
Tymvou **Vatili**
Agia **Kontea** Koukla
Arsos **Lysi** Kalopsida **Acheritou**
Margo **Tremetousia** **Makrasyka** Ag.Nikolaos
Pyrogi Melouseia **Achna** **Ypsoules**
Athienou **Pergamos** **Dasaki** **Frenaros** **Deryneia**
Troulloi **Xylotymvou** **Avgorou** **Sotira**
buroukina Avdellero **Pyla** **Ormideia** **Liopetri**
Kellia **Voroklini** **Xylofagou**
Kosi **Dekeleia**
Agia Anna **Livadia**
Kalo Chorio **Aradipou**
avdia **LARNAKA**
Dromolaxia **Larnaka International**
Alethriko **Meneou** Airport
Tersefanou **Kiti**
isides Kivisili
Aplanta **Perivolia**
afotida
Mazotos Cape Kiti

Paralimni

Protaras

Agia Napa

Cape Gkreko
(Pidalion)

Cape Pyla

AMMOCHOSTOS
BAY

AMMOCHOSTOS
(FAMAGUSTA)

Bogazi

Contents

introduction

Cyprus is the largest island in the eastern Mediterranean, comprising an area of 9,251 sq km within which lives a population of 749,200 inhabitants. The area of Cyprus is characterised by considerable diversity of scenery, ranging from flat plains a few metres above sea level, to lofty mountainous areas reaching a height of 1951 metres. A large number of geomorphologic features, like raised beaches, sea cliffs and sea caves, ravines and gorges, river captures, coastal sand dunes, beautiful tiny isles and, above all, fine and coarse-grained sandy beaches are encountered.

The natural vegetation, influenced by the island's position among three continents, is rich and varied with a number of endemic plants. Equally significant is the fauna of the island, with its unique moufflons roaming in herds in the forests of Pafos and Troodos. Moreover, millions of migratory birds use Cyprus as a stopover in their movement from the cold north-European countries to the warm countries of the African continent, and vice versa, during autumn, winter and spring.

What makes Cyprus a very attractive and fascinating country for the foreign visitor, however, is its long history, dating back to the neolithic times (7500 B.C.). The visitors can visit archaeological sites and museums, popular neighbourhoods and folk art museums, basilicas and Byzantine frescoed churches, traditional houses and wine-presses. They can walk over cobbled streets and medieval bridges, they can take part in local festivals and dance contests or they can watch or participate in the citrus, olive and grape gathering. Yet, if they like isolation, trekking, or countryside exploration, there are unspoilt areas, nature trails, large expanses of forest land and small, declining villages preserving their genuine customs and habits, particularly their hospitality.

It is not surprising that the fruitful Greek imagination, wise and infallible in all its creative conceptions, chose Cyprus, as the birthplace of the Goddess of Love and Beauty, a symbolical realization of the island's natural beauties and its poetic, romantic environment.

In this colourful guide we have selected the most important places of interest in the island which are well represented and illustrated. For visitors who need more information concerning other sites of interest we suggest the SELAS "Touring Guide of Cyprus", fully comprehensive guide with special and unique itineraries in the island.

Administratively Cyprus is divided into six districts (Lefkosia, Lemesos, Pafos, Larnaka, Ammochostos and Keryneia). Keryneia lies entirely in the occupied part of Cyprus, as do the biggest part of Ammochostos and a number of villages within the Lefkosia and Larnaka districts. In this guide you will find descriptions of the most important sites of interest within the area controlled by the government of the Republic of Cyprus.

Physical setting

The **climate** of Cyprus is mediterranean in character, with warm, dry summers and rainy, mild winters. Summer begins in mid-May and continues until the middle of September. Winter begins in November and continues until February. The average annual rainfall of Cyprus over the last 30 years is 503 mm. Snowfall is not a normal phenomenon in the plains, whereas on the Troodos massif snow can last for about 50 days a year. The rich **natural vegetation** of Cyprus is explained by its geographical position among three continents. The *forests* occupy 1,591.13 sq. km and represent 17.2% of the total area of the island. The main forest trees are the wild pine (Pinus brutia), the Troodos pine (Pinus nigra) and the cedars (Cedrus brevifolia) which are found in the Cedar Valley, Tripylos and other places. The *maquis* vegetation that grows mainly on siliceous soils, includes plants such as rose laurel, arbutus, myrtle, rosemary, etc. The *garrigue* which is a scrub vegetation grows mainly on limestone soils and includes such plants as lentisk, thyme and caper, as well as other aromatic xerophytes.

The same factors that influence the flora of the island are responsible for the **fauna** of Cyprus. The leading species of present-day fauna are the tame animals. The *moufflon,* which has lived in the forests of Cyprus since ancient times, is a variety of wild sheep and is currently the only large wild animal on the island. Cyprus is an ideal stopover for migratory birds. The Larnaka and Limassol lakes, for instance, attract a great number of migratory birds.

7

Left page:
Top: Dense forest around Platres
Bottom left: Giant fennel (Anathrika) from Kokkinochoria
Bottom right: Poppies in spring (Psevdas)

Top: Kalidonia Waterfalls (Lemesos District)

9

*Top left: Steatite idol of the chalcolithic period
(3000-2500 B.C.)
Top right: Copper ingot from Egkomi (1200 B.C.)
Bottom: "Combed ware" bowl from Choirokoitia
(4500-3700 B.C.)
(Photos, courtesy of the Dept. of Antiquities)*

Brief Historical survey of Cyprus

Cyprus has a long history dating back to the **Neolithic period** (7500-3900 B.C.). Neolithic settlements unearthed mainly in Choirokoitia and Kalavasos (Tenta) have revealed circular huts with corridors in between that were inhabited by early Cypriots, mainly engaged in farming, animal raising and hunting.

The **Chalcolithic period** (3900-2500 B.C.) is the precursor of copper discovery and the transitional stage from stone to copper. Among the chalcolithic settlements are those unearthed in Erimi (Lemesos district) and Lempa, Kissonerga and Souskiou (Pafos district).

The **Bronze Age** (2500-1050 B.C.) is adequately represented. During the early bronze age (2500-1900 B.C.), Lefkosia (Agia Paraskevi), Marki and Kotsiatis in the Lefkosia district were inhabited, whilst in the Pafos district, cemeteries of this age have been found at Kissonerga and Gialia. The middle bronze age (1900-1650 B.C.), a period of uncertainty, is represented by settlements such as Agios Sozomenos and Alampra in the Lefkosia district, Episkopi in Lemesos and Hala Sultan Tekke in Larnaka. The late bronze age (1650-1050 B.C.) is represented by Sotira, Alassa, Avdimou (Lemesos district), Agios Dimitrios Kalavasos, Maroni, Dromolaxia and Pyla in Larnaka district, and Palaepafos and Maa in the Pafos district. The late bronze age is particularly tranquil and prosperous, with considerable copper trade being carried out with other countries and Cypriot pottery and other forms of art being developed significantly. The late bronze age coincides with the arrival of the Myceneans (14th century B.C.). It is during this period that the Cypriot kingdoms such as Soloi, Chytroi, Idalio, Kourio, Golgoi and Salamis were founded by heroes of the Trojan War. Above all, the presence of the Myceneans (Achaeans) in Cyprus is associated with the Hellenization of the island. The Achaeans introduced to Cyprus a language, place names, institutions and cults.

Top: Three-footed vase with decoration of a horse (750-600 B.C.)
(Photo, courtesy of the Dept. of Antiquities)
Right: Bronze cauldron from Salamis (700 B.C.)

The **Iron Age**, a significant era starting about 1050 B.C. and coinciding with the beginning of the **Cypro-geometric period** (1050-750 B.C.), succeeded the late bronze age. The appearance of iron was a revolutionary invention, iron being harder and more durable than bronze. It is also during this period that the Phoenicians, well known tradesmen of antiquity, arrived in Cyprus, lured mainly by its copper ores and timber. Kition and Amathous were considered as having the strongest Phoenician character. The **Geometric** period obtained its name from the geometric shape of pottery and other works of art. During this period the Cypriot kingdoms, as many as twelve, were modelled on the Mycenean kingdoms. During the **Cypro-archaic period** (750-475 B.C.) Cyprus was conquered successively but always just for a short time by the Assyrians (673-669 B.C.), the Egyptians (560-545 B.C.) and the Persians (545-332 B.C.).

Apollo and Marsyas (4th c. A.D.)
(Photo, courtesy of the Dept. of Antiquities)

The **Classical period** (435-325 B.C.) coincides with the wars of the Greeks to liberate Cyprus from the Persians. Evagoras, united the kingdoms of Cyprus and fought for ten years against the Persians in an unequal conflict. Finally, he was forced to sign an agreement as king to king, abandoned all the Cypriot cities and accepted to pay tribute to the Persians. During the wars of Alexander the Great and his successive victories over the Persians, the Cypriots offered varied assistance to him, a gesture much appreciated. As a result, Alexander freed the island and the kings were left in undisputed possession.

The **Hellenistic period** (325-50 B.C.) starts in Cyprus after the death of Alexander the Great. His successors, Antigonus of Asia Minor and Ptolemy of Egypt, fought for the acquisition of Cyprus, with Ptolemy finally winning. It is during this period that the capital of Cyprus was transferred from Salamis to Pafos. The well-known Tombs of the Kings in Pafos is a remarkable monument of this period. The Theatre of Kourio, built in the 2nd century B.C. is an example of the significant cultural activity developed in Cyprus.

The **Roman period** (50 B.C.-330 A.D.) is marked by increased cultural development but also by disastrous earthquakes, droughts, etc. In Lemesos the Stadium of Kourio, the Theatre of Kourio (rebuilt and enlarged), the Sanctuary of Apollo (rebuilt) and some mosaics of Kourio are constructions of this period. In Pafos, the Mosaics, the Odeion, the Theatre, the Asklepieion and the Agora belong to the Roman period. In Agia Napa the Roman period is represented by the aqueduct, still visible at the monastery. It is during this period that Apostles Paul, Barnabas and his young relative Mark spread the Christian religion and succeeded in converting the proconsul Sergius Paulus to Christianity at Pafos. Cyprus became the first country in the world to be governed by a Christian.

During the **Byzantine period** (330-1191 A.D.) catastrophic earthquakes (332 A.D. and 342 A.D.) destroyed Salamis, Pafos and other cities. Salamis, under the name of Konstantia, was soon rebuilt and became the new capital of Cyprus. During the Arab raids, which lasted for almost three centuries, Cyprus suffered attacks, lootings and burnings with many of its settlements and churches destroyed. In 1185 Isaac Komninos, the Byzantine governor, declared himself independent ruler of Cyprus. Early Christian monasteries are those of Stavrovouni and Tochni constructed by Agia Eleni (St Helena), mother of Constantine the Great, who, according to tradition, on her return from the Holy Lands arrived in Cyprus. During the 11th century and immediately after, many of the well-known monasteries of Cyprus were built, including Kykkos, St John Chrysostomos, Machairas, St Neophytos (12th century), while many significant painted churches appeared, like Agios Nikolaos tis Stegis, Panagia tou Araka, Asinou, etc. Many of the nine churches in the Troodos area, included in the catalogue of world cultural heritage of UNESCO, belong to this period.

In 1191 A.D. Cyprus fell into the hands of **Richard the Lionheart,** king of England. Richard sold the island to the **Order of the Knights Templar** for 100,000 byzants. The Templars found the burden very heavy and thus Richard transferred sovereignty to Guy de Lusignan. Thus starts a 300-year Lusignan rule in Cyprus, known as the Frankish period.

During the **Frankish period** (1192-1489 A.D.), the feudal system of Medieval Europe was introduced to Cyprus. The Walls of Lefkosia and Ammochostos were constructed during this period. The last queen of Cyprus, Catherine Kornaro, yielded the island to the Venetians in 1489.

The Venetians who ruled Cyprus from 1489-1571 A.D. were conscious of the forthcoming Turkish invasion and hurriedly constructed the Lefkosia and Ammochostos walls. In the case of Lefkosia, the walls were smaller in circumference than the pre-existing Lusignan ones, with 11 bastions and three gates. Currently, the walls of Lefkosia and the gates, particularly Ammochostos Gate, constitute the most significant relics of the Venetian period. Towers were also constructed as observatories at Xylofagou, Pyla, Kiti and Alaminos in the Larnaka district, while the castle of Kyrenia was strengthened. Furthermore, the Venetians exploited further the salt

Fresco from the Byzantine church of Panagia Araka

Left page:
Top: Panagia Forviotissa (1105 A.D. wall painting), Asinou
Bottom left: The Angel from the scene of the Annunciation (1192 A.D.),
Panagia Araka, Lagoudera
Bottom right: Pantokrator (1332/3 A.D.), Panagia Araka, Lagoudera
(Photos, courtesy of the Dept. of Antiquities)

The hoisting of the British flag in Lefkosia (engraving)

production from the Salt Lake of Larnaka. Despite the fortifications, Turkey successfully attacked Cyprus.

The Turkish rule (1571-1878 A.D.) was characterized by oppressive taxes, misgovernment, a decline of trade and productivity as well as a decrease in population. Earthquakes, epidemics and plagues of locusts were also a feature of the period. During the Turkish rule Cyprus was divided into six districts with 17 departments (katilikia). It is during this period that many Christian cathedrals and chapels were converted into mosques, such as Agia Sofia in Nicosia and Agios Nikolaos at Famagusta. The establishment of khans and public baths (hamam) was another feature of the period, while some fortification works were executed such as the reconstruction of the Pafos castle, etc.

The British Administration lasted for 82 years (1878-1960 A.D.). The administration of Cyprus was transferred to Great Britain after an agreement between Great Britain and Turkey. In 1914 the island was annexed and after all rights and claims to the island were renounced by Turkey, Cyprus was declared a Crown Colony in 1925.

Between 1955 and 1959 Cyprus experienced its Liberation Struggle for the Union of Cyprus with Greece. It was a centuries' old ardent desire which culminated in conflict between the Greek Cypriots and the British. Finally the Zurich-London Agreements of 1959 established the Cyprus Republic. On 16th August 1960 Cyprus was declared an independent republic.

The real development of Cyprus was achieved after Independence (1960). The population of Cyprus increased significantly and services multiplied. However, the Turkish invasion of 1974 had as a result the occupation of a large number of settlements in the northern part of the island, the inhabitants of which are currently displaced in the free part of Cyprus.

Lefkosia town

Left page: Eleftheria Square

Top: Konstantinos Palaiologos street parallel to the walls of Lefkosia

Lefkosia (Nicosia), the largest town of Cyprus, has been the capital of the island since Medieval times. The history of the city is both interesting and adventurous. In the area known today as Prodromos, on the left bank of the Pediaios river, a number of artifacts dating from the **Chalcolithic period** (3900 B.C.) were discovered, leading us to believe that here was the precursor of the contemporary Lefkosia. During the **early Bronze Age** (2500-1900 B.C.), three settlements were founded in the broader Lefkosia urban area: "Leondari Vouno" in Athalassa, Agia Paraskevi and Lefkosia proper. The two main factors contributing to the establishment of the Lefkosia settlement were the presence of water from the Pediaios river and the fertile land, which favoured the development of agriculture and animal husbandry. During the **Roman period** it was a small and insignificant agricultural settlement. Until the **Byzantine period,** more specifically until the 4th century AD, the settlement is referred to as Ledrae. During this period the constant Arab raids cause worries and fear along

the coast leading to the abandonment of several settlements, whose residents seek safety further inland. During the Byzantine period Lefkosia becomes the capital of Cyprus, a function it maintains to this day. Towards the end of the Byzantine period, Lefkosia falls to Richard the Lionheart (1191) following his victory over Isaakios Comninos, the Byzantine governor of Cyprus, at Tremetousia. In 1192, Richard sells the island to Guy de Lusignan, founder of the same-named dynasty. During the **Frankish period** (1192-1489) Lefkosia becomes the administrative centre of the island and a number of nobles set up home here, while at the same time the city is adorned with imposing buildings and churches, such as the Church of Agia Sofia. During the Lusignan era Lefkosia is fortified by walls which have since been replaced by the Venetian walls. It is during this same period that the city is renamed Nicosia, possibly because the Frankish invaders had difficulty pronouncing the Greek name "Lefkosia". The **Venetian era** (1489-1571) was marked

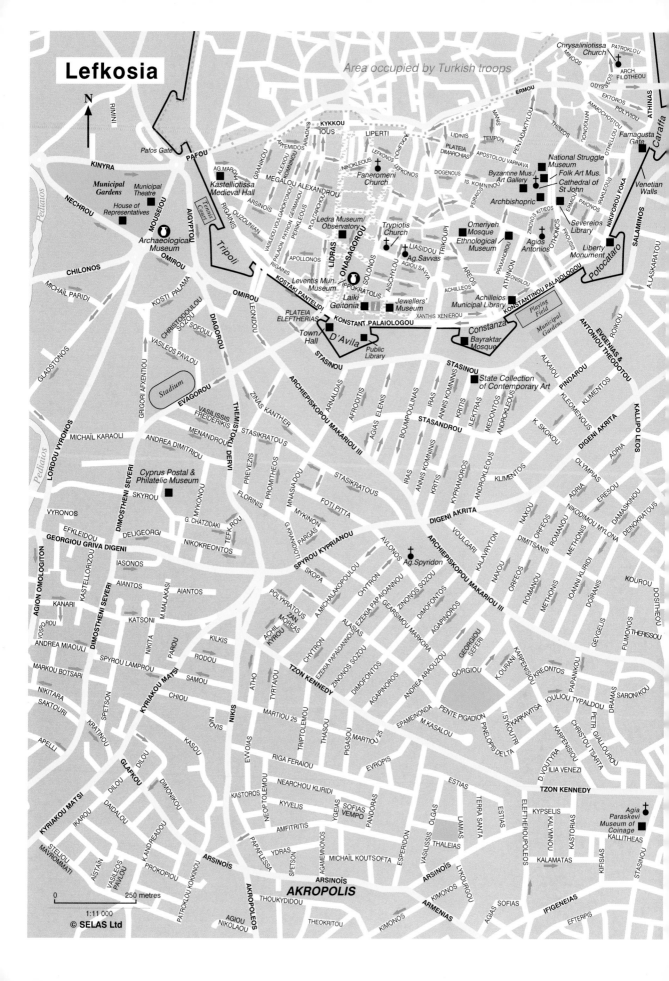

Medieval Lefkosia within the Venetian walls (engraving)

by the construction of the walls, which enclosed a smaller area than the walls erected by the Lusignans. The new walls had three main portals, those of Ammochostos, Keryneia and Pafos. It is also during this period that the Pediaios river was diverted. During the **Ottoman rule** in Cyprus (1571-1878) Lefkosia remained the official capital of Cyprus. The heavy taxation and the economic decline, however, created a poor city with slow growth and an oriental mentality. The cultural and intellectual fields went into decline. Apart from the conversion of the Latin churches to mosques (e.g. Agia Sofia) and the creation of inns and baths, during this period the roads of Lefkosia were narrow and earthen. During **British Colonial rule** (1878-1960), Lefkosia continued to be the capital of Cyprus. The Presidential Palace was constructed in 1878 at the imposing and strategic position it holds today. During this period Lefkosia expanded beyond its walls. Furthermore, during British rule, the road network was expanded and Lefkosia was now not only linked to Larnaka by carriageway but with other regions of Cyprus as well. All this resulted in the rapid growth of Lefkosia's population and consequently the increased need for housing. Following **Independence** (1960), Lefkosia's population increased mainly due to the trend to move to the cities and the concentration of economic, administrative, educational and other activities in the city. After 1963, the capital was divided, initially with the formation of a sizeable Turkish enclave and later on account of the Turkish invasion of 1974, which led to a complete division of the city. The Turkish invasion struck a serious blow to the capital, leading to the loss of the Mia Milia industrial area, the closing of the international airport, the creation of the buffer zone, something which deprived Greek Cypriots of a significant housing area. Despite all the adversities, Lefkosia continued to grow. It is now a financial centre and a popular venue for local and international conferences and activities.

Archaeological sites and cultural monuments

The Walls of Lefkosia. The Venetian Walls of Lefkosia, were constructed between 1567 and 1570. The original Lusignan Walls, protecting a wider area, were demolished and their building material was used to construct the Venetian Walls, 4.83km long with 11 heart-shaped bastions at regular intervals of 280m. There were three gates: The Pafos Gate (Porta di San Domenico, in the south-west), the Keryneia Gate (Porta del Provveditore, in the north) and the Ammochostos (Famagusta) Gate (Porta Giuliana, in the east). The circular Walls of Lefkosia have been described as an achievement of architectural design for the 16th century. In recent times, the moat has been transformed into public gardens, car parks, playgrounds, etc.

Famagusta Gate was originally called Porta Giuliana in honour of Giulio Savorgnano. It was named Famagusta Gate due to the fact that the gate lies east of the walls and served mainly the roads from the Famagusta and Larnaka districts. The Famagusta Gate is considered to be the best Venetian monument surviving in Lefkosia. The inner side of the gate facing the city is very imposing with an arched door, two oval windows and marble coats of arms on the facade. The entire building consists of a vaulted passage with a spherical dome in the centre which admits sunlight inside. On both sides run two parallel large rooms. In 1930 the Municipality of Lefkosia established a nearby opening of the walls, thus preventing the passage of people, animals and vehicles through the "true" gate of Famagusta. The transformation of Famagusta Gate into the Nicosia Municipal Cultural Centre dates from 1981. In 1984 it was awarded the Europa Nostra prize. Currently the Famagusta Gate is used for lectures, art and book exhibitions, theatrical performances and for many other artistic and intellectual activities.

Laiki Geitonia (Popular neighbourhood). The Laiki Geitonia quarter, restored by the Municipality of Lefkosia in 1983, is about 1,600 sq. metres and lies within the walls, close to Eleftheria square. Traditional houses of the 19th and early 20th century have either been restored or constructed in such a way as to preserve the physiognomy of that period. Visitor can enjoy paved narrow streets, traditional houses built with hewn limestone blocks, arches, arcades, two-storeyed houses, carved margins around the doors and the windows, pebble-paved paths, wooden balconies, old lanterns, etc. Inside the houses, wood beams and straw mat ceilings supported by thin trunks of pine trees are the predominant features. Restaurants, boutiques, galleries as well as various craftsmen's workshops can be found along the narrow paved narrow streets.

Left page: Laiki Geitonia (Popular neighbourhood) by night

Bottom: Famagusta Gate

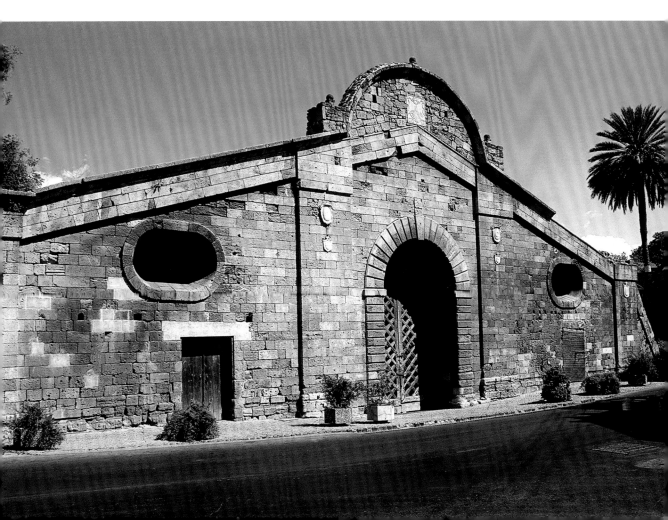

Top: The Archbishopric Palace
Left: The House of Hadjigeorgakis Kornesios

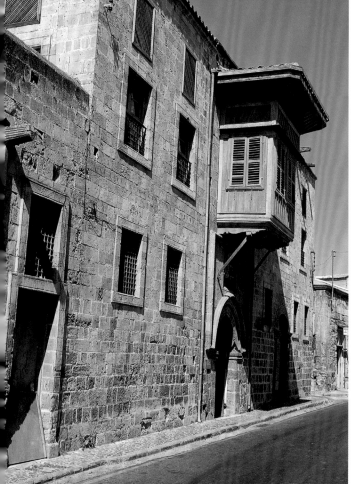

The Archbishopric. The Archbishop's Palace is an impressive modern building in Byzantine style, built between 1956 and 1960. The old Archbishopric, close by, houses the Folk Art Museum. The Archbishopric is the residence of the Archbishop and the headquarters of the Cyprus Orthodox Church. The two-storeyed building with a tiled roof, constructed with hewn limestone blocks, houses a large number of icons, manuscripts and other treasures of the Cyprus Church. Many additions to the whole structure took place between 1976 and 1987, when the Archbishop Makarios III Foundation was establlished, currently housing, among others, the Art Gallery and the Byzantine Museum. At the front of the building stands, since 1987, a gigantic bronze statue of Makarios, cast by sculptor N. Kotchamanis. At the other end of the Palace is a bust of Archbishop Kyprianos, executed by the Turks in 1821.

The reception room (oda) of the Hadjigeorgakis Kornesios House (Photo, courtesy of the Dept. of Antiquities)

Ethnological Museum (Hadjigeorgakis Kornesios House). Close to the Archbishopric stands the two-storeyed, stone-built mansion of Hadjigeorgakis Kornesios, a famous dragoman (liaison between the Turkish Government and the Greek community) from 1779 to 1809. The house of Hadjigeorgakis Kornesios constitutes the most important building of urban architecture of the 18th century. The entrance is through a carved arched door above which a coat of arms portrays the double-headed eagle and the lion of Venice. The arches, the columns that support the first floor, the marble slabs covering the floor, the cobbledstone paths of the ground floor, as well as the stable and the rooms for the household staff are other features of the house. A wide staircase leads to the first floor where the reception room (oda) impresses with its decoration and content.

The Liberty Monument

The Liberty Monument. The marble Monument of Liberty, inspired and created by Notaras, lies on a bastion of the medieval walls. Though the monument was erected in 1970, ten years after the independence of Cyprus, it vivifies the heroic efforts of the Struggle of Liberation (1955-59) and immortalises the entire psychological and sentimental world of Cyprus, marked by centuries of slavery, martyrdom, perseverence and hope. The Goddess Liberty dominates the highest point of the composition, casting her glance at the two soldiers who open the door of a prison. Fourteen persons, representing different types of Cypriots, from all strata of life, emerge from the narrow dark prison and gaze at the light of sun and liberty.

Museums and Galleries

The Archaeological Museum of Lefkosia. A civilization of 9,500 years in condensed format is exhibited in the 14 rooms of the Archaeological Museum, built in 1908. *Room 1* contains finds from the Neolithic period (7500-3900 B.C.) and the Chalcolithic era (3900-2500 B.C.) including decorated pottery. *Room 2* covers the Early Bronze Age (2500-1900 B.C.) and shows evidence of an economy based on copper production. *Room 3* exhibits pottery of the Middle (1900-1650 B.C.) and Late Bronze Age (1650-1050 B.C.) and vases from the Mycenean to the Roman period. In *Room 4* about 2000 terracotta figurines found in Agia Eirini Sanctuary and dating from 700 B.C. are exhibited. In *Room 5* one sees the evolution of Cypriot sculpture on clay, stone and bronze; a limestone head from Arsos and a Hellenistic Aphrodite from Soloi dominate the exhibits of the room. In *Room 6* there are various Roman bronzes, the sleeping Eros from Pafos and a superb nude bronze of Emperor Septimius Severus. *Room 7* is devoted to metallurgy. Copper utensils, varied bronze objects as well as ivory artifacts, glassware, scarabs, coins from the Cypriot kingdoms and the mosaic of Leda and the Swan are in the room. *Room 8* contains interesting reconstructions of tombs while *Room 9* contains tombstones, stylae, capitals, sarcophagi from the Hellenistic period, etc. *Room 10* introduces the visitor to the world of inscriptions where examples of Cypro-minoic as well as ancient Cypriot syllabary are exhibited. The precious objects found at Salamis and notably the famous bronze cauldron with its iron tripod are exhibited in *Room 11*. *Room 12* has seen the recent addition of objects of ancient metallurgy, while *Room 13* exhibits the marble statue of Asklepios, the marble statue of Aphrodite and the statue of Apollo. In *Room 14* there are a large number of clay idols.

The Byzantine Museum of the Makarios III Foundation. The Byzantine Museum hosts icons spanning the millennium from the 8th to the 18th century. The oldest painting is one of the Virgin Mary, using encaustic technique characteristic of the 8th and 9th centuries, whereby molten wax was mixed in with colours. The Museum hosts many icons dating from the 12th century, a time when iconography is considered to have reached its zenith. The 13th century is typified by the polymorphous technique, a technique which extended to later centuries as well. The oblong icons, depicting Jesus, Agios Eleftherios and Agia Paraskevi date from the 14th century and come from the Chrysaliniotissa church. The icon of the Virgin Mary is

Apollo holding a lyre (Lefkosia Archaeological Museum)

Top left: Bronze statue of Septimios Seviros
Top right: Marble statue of Aphrodite from Soloi (1st c.B.C.)
(Lefkosia Archaeological Museum)

Bottom left: Wood-carved armoire, Folk Art Museum (Photo, courtesy of the Folk Art Museum)
Bottom right: Entry into Jerusalem from the church of Virgin Chrysaliniotissa (Photo, courtesy of Arch. Makarios III Foundation)

The Old Archbishopric

from the church of Faneromeni in Lefkosia. Among the most impressive icons of the 15th century is the double-faced icon of the Virgin Mary and the Lowering from the Cross, from the Church of Agia Marina in Kalopanagiotis. Many icons date back to the 16th century.

The Art Gallery of Makarios III Foundation. At the eastern end of the imposing Archbishopric is the Art Gallery of the Cultural Centre of the Archbishop Makarios III Foundation. The inauguration of the Cultural Centre was held on January 18, 1982, when the Gallery was opened to the public. The first floor of the Gallery features 116 European oil paintings, dating from the 16th to the 19th centuries, dominated by scenes from religion and mythology. A number of European schools of art are represented here, such as the French, Italian, Spanish, Flemish, German and others. The second floor features approximately 80 oil paintings by European artists, inspired mainly from Greek history, more specifically the Greek Revolution of 1821.

Folk Art Museum. The Lefkosia Folk Art Museum is housed in the old Archbishopric and belongs to the Society of Cypriot Studies which was founded in 1937. Its rich exhibits bear witness to the internal world, the intellectual life, the aesthetic criteria and the inventiveness of the Cypriot artisan. The variety of the exhibits, the shapes, colours, harmony and adornment express the struggle and the faith of the Cypriot people with respect to life itself. Here one sees aspects of bygone eras through pottery, weaving, basket-making, silver and goldsmithery, sculpture, etc. In a semi-covered area, one can see, among others, large, red jars, hand-driven mills, ploughs, cereal-threshing implements, an olive press and a wooden waterwheel.

The National Struggle Museum. In 1961, one year after the independence of Cyprus, the National Struggle Museum was established. The Museum, housed in the old Archbishopric, aims to preserve the memory of the struggle for liberation. The Museum contains photos of almost all events of the "Struggle Period" (1955-59), letters and personal belongings of the freedom fighters, military equipment, representations of hide-outs and fights, as well as a large number of other documents.

Top: Leventis Municipal Museum

Right page: Service outside the Cathedral of St John the Theologian

Leventis Municipal Museum. In 1989, the Leventis Municipal Museum was founded at Ippokratis Street, within the walls of Lefkosia. Housed in a two-storeyed, 19th century home, the museum exhibits photos, engravings, Venetian coins, Byzantine pottery and icons, coins of Byzantine emperors, pottery from the Bronze and Iron Age, etc.

Cyprus Jewellers' Museum. Goldsmithing and silversmithing are two very ancient trades, as testified, by archaeological finds. The Cyprus Jewellers' Museum at Laiki Geitonia displays jewellery as from the last century. The visitor can observe ornaments, religious items, silver and gold items and a multitude of other objects.

The Cathedral of Agios Ioannis Theologos (Saint John the Theologian), situated between the old and the new archbishopric, is possibly the best known church in the island. Prior to the 18th century, the present-day Cathedral was the church of the monastery of St John Pipis, dating from medieval times. Following its destruction and according to an inscription above the western entrance, Archbishop Nikiforos rebuilt it in 1662. The paintings of the cathedral, probably undertaken between 1735 and 1763, are the work of Archbishop Filotheos. Inside the church one is impressed by the frescoes and the finely-carved wooden iconostasis, which is adorned with numerous representations of animals, plants, birds, etc. What stands out is a double row of portable icons that depict the life of Christ.

Lefkosia countryside

Top: Galata and part of Kakopetria village
Left: Church of Panagia Podithou (Galata)

Galata is famous for its traditional architecture of wooden balconies and wooden staircases and its medieval churches. The churches of Agia Paraskevi, Agios Georgios and Agios Nikolaos unfortunately have lost their paintings. However, the frescoes of the churches of Archangelos Michail, Panagia Podithou and Agios Sozomenos are rich and attract numerous visitors.

The single-aisled, timber-roofed *church of Archangelos Michail*, also known as church of Panagia Theotokos, is painted completely in the post-Byzantine style of the early sixteenth century.

Close to the church of Archangelos Michail lies the *church of Panagia Podithou,* of the steep-pitched-roof type, with ventilators recently opened on the roof. It was originally a small monastery. The church was erected in 1502 A.D.

The church of Agios Sozomenos in the middle of the old settlement is of the steep-pitched-roof type with an enclosure added later. The church was restored in 1963, and its paintings belong to the post-Byzantine school of painting. The church was erected in 1513.

Top: Church of Agios Nikolaos tis Stegis
Right: Entry into Jerusalem, fresco from the church of Agios Nikolaos tis Stegis (Photo, courtesy of the Archaeological Museum)

Kakopetria is surrounded by green orchards and lush vegetation. Tall alder, plane and poplar-trees grow on the banks of the Kargotis river. The western part of the settlement is more compact, with narrow, meandering streets. The two-storeyed houses have steep-pitched roofs, while the balconies and tiled roofs are made of wood. This is the older part of Kakopetria with its traditional architecture. In contrast, the eastern part consists of modern, more spacious houses which do not differ much from the houses in the towns. The well-known water-mill of Kakopetria, about 800m from the village square, has functioned as from the 18th century until recently. Though Kakopetria boasts three painted churches (Agios Nikolaos tis Stegis, Panagia Theotokos and Agios Georgios Perachoritis), the church of Agios Nikolaos is strongly recommended. It was built in the 11th century, while the domed narthex was added in the 12th century. The church constituted part of a monastery which was dissolved, most probably in the second half of the 19th century. The church is adorned entirely with frescoes ranging from the 11th to the 17th century. In the 13th century the steep-pitched roof was added to protect the church from rain and snow.

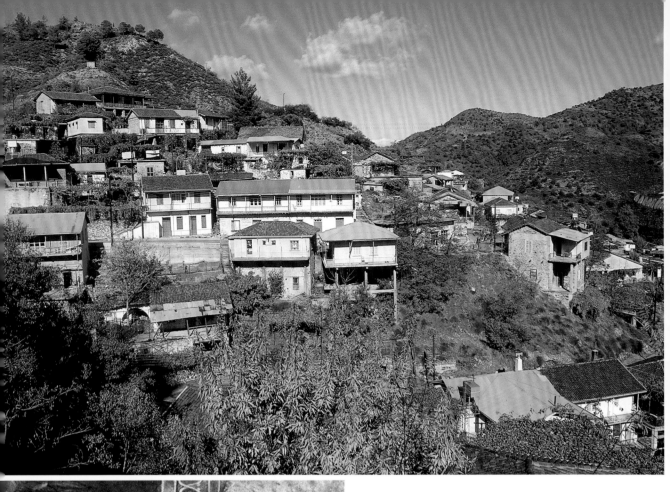

Top: Kalopanagiotis village
Left: Crucifixion (Monastery of Agios Ioannis Lampadistis, 13th c. A.C.)

Right page:
Top: Kalopanagiotis dam in autumn
Bottom: Pedoulas village

Kalopanagiotis has a rich traditional architecture, mainly winding streets, two-storeyed houses with balconies and climbing vines. There are many chapels and churches in the village, including the very significant ancient monastery of Agios Ioannis Lampadistis. The disused monastery of Agios Ioannis Lampadistis is currently a complex of several buildings from several periods. The main buildings are: (i) the cross-in-square church of Agios Irakleidios to the south, dating back to the eleventh century; (ii) the vaulted church of Agios Ioannis Lampadistis in the middle, probably of the 12th century and restored in the 18th c. In the church, the skull of the Saint is preserved in a silver casket; (iii) a common narthex attached to the west end of the two churches, timber-roofed, of the 15th century; (iv) a tall vaulted building to the north, built in the 15th century possibly as a Latin chapel.

Top: Moutoullas village

Right page:
Top: Panagia Asinou church
Bottom: Dormition of the Virgin (12 c. wall painting), Asinou

Moutoullas. The traditional architecture of Moutoullas with narrow, winding cobbledstone streets, the steep-pitched roofs and large wooden balconies, as well as the carved doors and windows with climbing vines at the main entrance, is indeed interesting. The most significant site of interest is the church of Panagia of Moutoullas situated in the upper part of the village. The church has a steep-pitched roof and was built in 1280.

Pedoulas is a compact settlement with buildings standing on narrow terraces, one above the other. The climbing vines in nearly every house yard are part of the traditional architecture. Vrysin is a beautiful, enchanting site where abundant water gushes out from the mountainside and where a restaurant-café caters for people seeking tranquility and summer coolness. The village is crowned with a gigantic cross, about 20 m high, close to an arched chapel. The dominant feature of the settlement is the large domed church of the Holy Cross with its two belfries in the middle of the village. Pedoulas is currently a summer resort with a number of small hotels. The most significant site of interest, however, is the church of Archangelos Michail, a painted steep-pitched church in the lower part of the village dating back to 1474.

The Byzantine church of Panagia Asinou is located about 5 km south of Nikitari village. It is probable that at the same locality there existed a monastery, known as Monastery of Forviotissa, which was dissolved during the Ottoman rule. The single-aisled church, built with local stone, is supported by arched recesses. Most probably the 12th century church had a dome, which collapsed and was replaced by an arch. The narthex at the west end was added in the 12th century. The whole structure is covered with a second steep-pitched roof with flat tiles. It is, however, the interior of the church that fascinates with its superb frescoes dating from the early 12th century onwards.

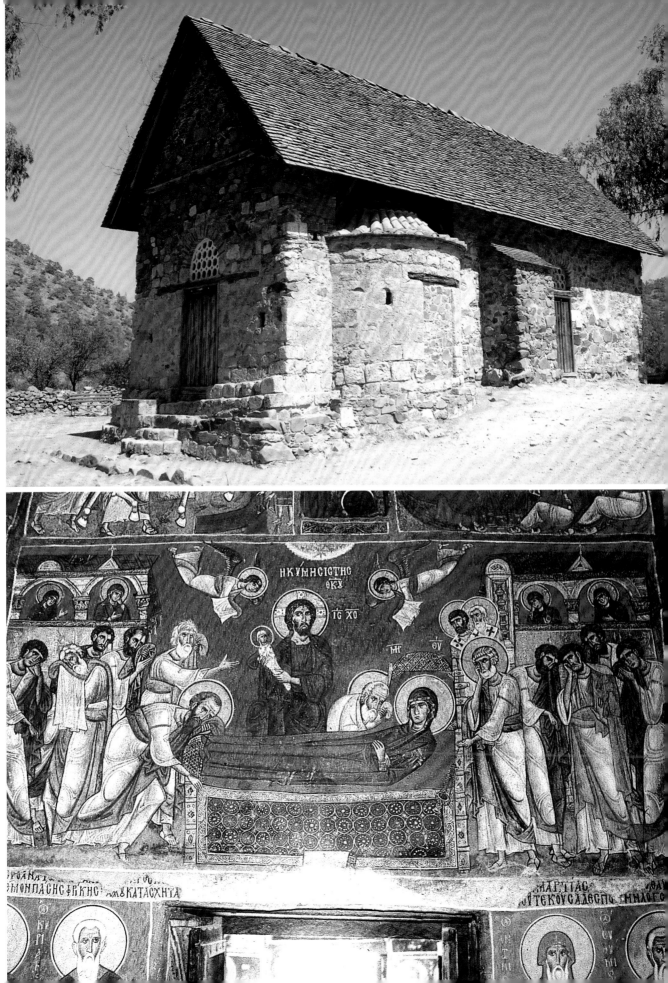

Top: Fikardou village

Right page: Monastery of Machairas

The traditional architecture of **Fikardou** is remarkable, with narrow, winding streets, houses of the steep-pitched type and wood-carved doors and windows, some dating back to the 18th/19th centuries. Fikardou has been much publicized in recent years because it has been declared a monument and was awarded the EUROPA NOSTRA prize. Two houses have been restored and currently constitute living folk art museums: *The house of Katsiniorou,* a two-storeyed building of the 16th century with a steep-pitched roof, constructed with local building materials. The visitor can see the large wine jars, the stable, the loom and many other utensils of every day use. A second two-storeyed house restored by donation of the *Leventis Foundation,* has many exhibits from the 19th century and is worth visiting.

Machairas Monastery (Panagia Machairiotissa), at 1,425m above sea level, is one of the most famous monasteries of Cyprus. According to tradition, the monastery was founded around 1145 A.D. by hermits Neofytos and Ignatios, who had been expelled from Syria. The two hermits discovered the icon of Madonna in a cave and a knife near by. Most probably the monastery's name is derived from the word machaira, meaning knife in Greek. It is believed that the miraculous icon has been painted by Apostle Luke. Emperor Emmanuel Komninos provided funds towards the establishment of the monastery around 1172 A.D. Originally a chapel with a few cells were constructed, while later Nilos, the abbot, built the church and the cells of the monastery with a surrounding wall. The monastery has experienced many vicissitudes and persecutions ever since. It was completely destroyed in 1530 as well as in 1892. In both cases, by miracle, the icon of the Virgin Mary was saved. The present three-aisled church of Machairas was built between 1500 and 1892. The rest of the buildings were constructed after the fire of 1892. Visitors are impessed by the two mosaic-compositions right and left of the main entrance, depicting the privileges of the monastery and the discovery of the icon of Virgin Mary.

Top: Stavros tou Agiasmati church
Left: Panagia Arakiotissa, 12th c. A.D. wall painting, Lagoudera
(Photo, courtesy of the Dep. of Antiquities)

The church of Stavros tou Agiasmati (Holy Cross of Agiasmati). Following a winding, earthen road, about 3 km north of Platanistasa village, the visitor can reach the isolated medieval church of Stavros tou Agiasmati. The nearby spring of water is as old as the church, which in the 15th century was part of a monastery. The foundations of the cells are still visible. The frescoes and paintings of the church are very impressive. Visitors should focus their attention on the Birth of Christ, Baptism, The Last Supper, the Betrayal, the Washing of the Feet, the Denial of Peter, the Mocking, the Lamentation, the Dormition of the Mother of God, etc. In the bema Virgin Mary is one of the finest paintings of the church. The frescoes of Stavros tou Agiasmati (15th century), constitute a transitory stage from the Byzantine to the Rennaissance Art.

Lagoudera is famous for its Byzantine church, known as **Panagia of Araka.** The domed church, of the 12th century A.D., is single-aisled with three arched recesses in the side walls. The building is covered with a later steep-pitched roof which extends to a later enclosure. The interior of the church is completely covered with paintings of the mid-Byzantine period. Impressive frescoes are Christ Pantokrator looking down from the dome with detached serenity, the presentation of the Virgin Mary to the Temple, the Birth of Christ, the Baptism, the Crucifixion and the Ascension of Christ. The Dormition of the Holy Mother of God is regarded as a masterpiece of Byzantine art. In the bema, where frescoes are preserved in vivid colours, the visitor can see the Virgin Mary enthroned with Christ seated in her lap, attended by archangels Gabriel and Michael. The guilted iconostasis dates from 1673.

The **Cedar Valley** and **Tripylos** are two distinctive areas where the visitor can enjoy cedar trees (Cedrus brevifolia). Though these areas are within the Pafos forest, administratively they belong to the Lefkosia district. The best route to reach **Cedar Valley** is from Kykko monastery towards Tsakistra. Before approaching Tsakistra, visitors can follow the earthen forest road to the left and, at the junction of the roads leading to the Pafos forest they should follow the road towards Panagia. Cedars appear at the beginning mixed with other forest trees, while later a whole valley is covered with cedar trees with their branches appearing as carpets the one above the other. Cedar-trees around **Tripylos** are denser than in the Cedar Valley. One can reach Tripylos by taking the road from Kykko Monastery towards Tsakistra and following the first earthen forest road to the left towards Stavros tis Psokas. The feeling is that of a gigantic umbrella placed on the slopes of Tripylos and stretching for a few kilometres.

Cedar valley

Left page: Monastery of Kykkos

Top: Entrance to the Monastery of Kykkos

Kykkos Monastery. Situated at about 1,150 metres a.s.l., Kykkos monastery is the most renowned monastery in Cyprus and well-known throughout the Orthodox world. The fame of the monastery throughout Orthodoxy is mainly due to the icon of the Virgin Mary, housed in the monastery, and believed to be painted by St. Luke. The icon, one of three painted by St. Luke while the Mother of Christ was alive, is much venerated by Cypriots, who visit the monastery and pray to the icon regularly. The monastery is of Byzantine origin, founded by Isaias, a hermit, probably at the end of the 11th century, during the reign of Alexios Komninos. Isaias with the help of the Virgin Mary cured Voutomitis, the duke of Cyprus, of sciatica. Voutomitis subsequently announced the miracle to Alexios Komninos whose daughter suffered from the same disease. Finally the Byzantine Emperor agreed to give the real icon of the Virgin Mary, demanded by Isaias, in order to save his daughter. Thus, the icon of Eleousa as it is known ended up at Kykko, and the first monastery was built. Though the monastery was burned several times, in 1365, in 1541, in 1751 and in 1813, the miraculous icon unscathed. The icon for centuries has been considered too sacred to gaze upon, and is silver-covered since 1576. The icon enjoys a great reputation among Cypriots as rain bearing. The three-aisled church, with its impressive iconostasis, is decorated with frescoes. The frescoes have been extended even outside the church. The library of the monastery is rich with very old ecclesiastical books and manuscripts. The recently inaugurated Kykkos Museum is very imposing, contributing to the intellectual and cultural life of Cyprus and preserves works of art as old as 900 years ago. The museum comprises many priceless relics, such as carved ivory plaques, reliquaries, gospels, carved wooden crosses, etc.

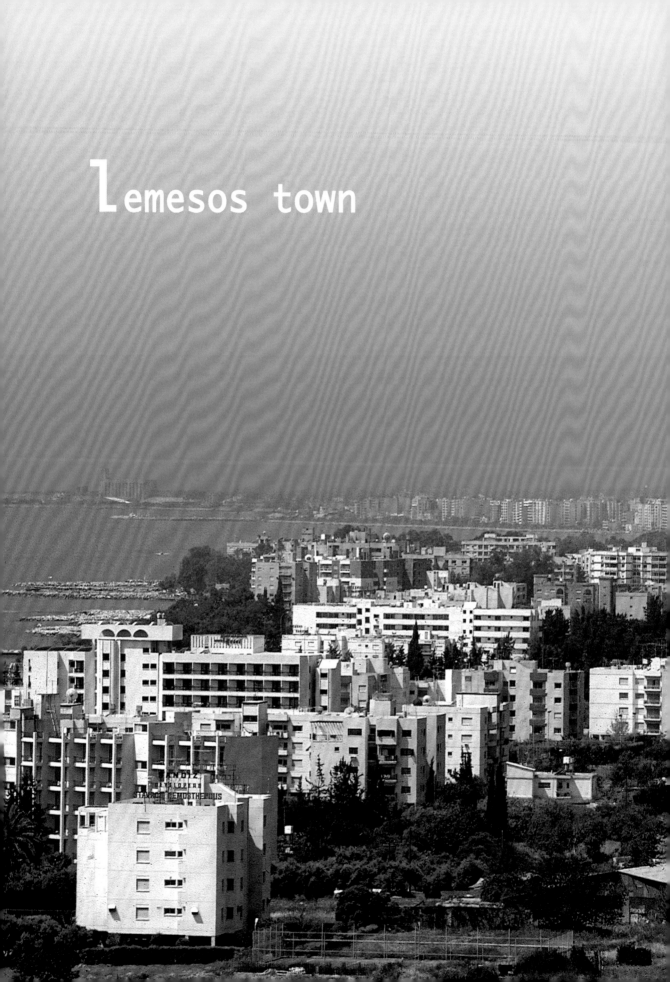

Lemesos town

Left page: View of Lemesos town

Top: Old pier (Lemesos old port)

It is still not known when Lemesos (Limassol) was built and what its initial name was. Situated between the two ancient kingdoms of Kourio and Amathous, it may not have been able to spread and grow in population while these two cities still flourished. It appears that during the pre-Christian era, there existed a small settlement, the name of which is unknown, whose dwellers were farmers and fishermen. The history of Lemesos is undoubtedly established with the arrival, in Cyprus, of King Richard the Lionheart (Coeur de Lion) of England, during the Third Crusade. The marriage of Richard to Berengaria at the chapel of St George, the battle of Tremetousia between the armies of Richard and Komninos, the defeat and capture of the latter, the total destruction of Amathous (1191 A.D.) and the bolstering of the population of Lemesos, were the basic factors that contributed to the city's independent and dynamic rise. During the Frankish period (1192-1489 A.D.), Lemesos becomes the seat of a Latin bishop, which was maintained until the Turkish conquest of the island in 1571. The fall of Acra drove away a number of monastic orders, among which the Knights Templar and the Knights of St John, which arrived in Lemesos during the 13th century. Many Venetians settled in Cyprus, particularly in Lemesos, where they established them-selves predominantly as traders. In 1221, the city of Lemesos suffered a raid by the Saracens, resulting in thousands of dead, wounded and captives. One year later, Lemesos was struck by an earthquake. In 1330, the Garyllis river burst its banks, causing great damage to Lemesos. Later in 1373, Lemesos was set ablaze by the Genoese, and again in 1408. The Egyptian Mamelukes attacked Cyprus, focusing on Lemesos since the city was considered a haven for the pirates who scourged the Eastern Mediterranean. The Venetians (1489-1571) were not interested in fortifying Lemesos, since they were expecting a Turkish attack, that did not last long. Once again during the Venetian period, Lemesos was hit by earthquakes and became the target of numerous Turkish raids, prior to the massive Turkish attack of 1571. During the Turkish occupancy (1571-1878), Lemesos was, according to foreign visitors, "a miserable village". Some mention the carob trade which was carried out through its port, while others attributed its adverse conditions to the administration and the lootings perpetrated by the occupying Turkish forces. It is, however, mentioned that during this period the Latin Church was ousted and Orthodoxy was restored. Furthermore, during the Turkish occupation, a number of inns and camel sheds

The Medieval castle of Lemesos

were set up in Lemesos, whose presence continued for a number of years after the arrival of the British in Cyprus. The British colonial period (1878-1960) was marked by a gradual improvement in the standard of living, the paving of roads, the expansion of the city's commercial and industrial activities, the establishment of a pier for on and off loading at the port, street-lighting, the advancement (to a small extent) of the hotel business and the setting-up of necessary services, such as the hospital, post office, etc. The development, however, of private initiative, especially among Lemesos' intellectuals, businessmen and scientists, contributed to the gradual improvement of almost all sectors of activity from the beginning of the British colonial period to the outset of the Independence of Cyprus. Following the independence and the establishment of the Republic of Cyprus (1960), Lemesos began to grow, both in area and population. After the Turkish invasion of 1974, Lemesos port took over the role of the port of Famagusta and is now the major port of Cyprus. The establishment of secondary, tourist-related activities, contributed to the development of tourism in the region.

The Medieval Castle. The castle, only a short distance from the old port, was probably built during the 13th century. The original form of the castle is not known since it has suffered repeated destruction by the Genoese, the Mamelukes and, later on, the Turks. In 1525, the Venetian governor of Cyprus, Fransesco Bragadino, ordered the blowing-up and destruction of the castle, upon its being seized by Turkish pirates. The castle was restored during the 14th century, as well as towards the end of the 15th or beginning of the 16th century. Both the 1491 earthquake and the many raids contributed to major alterations to its initial design. The grand Gothic hall in the basement is particularly impressive, featuring elegant semi-domes and pillars. A narrow corridor links this hall to a small, domed chapel, framed by two other small and domed compartments. These may be traces of the original castle. According to tradition, this is where Richard the Lionheart's wedding to Berengaria of Navarro was performed in 1191, when the then King of England conquered Cyprus. The Castle of Lemesos has recently been enriched with a large number of medieval objects and is now known as the Medieval Castle.

Top left: Vessel with decoration (Sotira), 4500-3750 B.C.
Bottom left: Head of Lavranios Zeus

Top right: Jug from Amathus, 6th c. B.C.
Bottom right: Red-polished vase from Polemidia (2000-1850 B.C.)
(Photos, courtesy of the Dept. of Antiquities)

Photos from the Folk Art Museum of Lemesos

Museums

The Archaeological Museum of Lemesos houses a rich and notable collection of antiquities, covering all the significant periods of Cypriot history. The exhibits are housed in three relatively spacious rooms and are divided into three main categories. One room primarily contains pottery of significant historical periods, the middle room houses an exhibition of coins, jewellery, lamps and a variety of copper tools and wares, while the third hosts sculptures, tombstones, capitals, inscriptions, a sarcophagus, as well as other marble and local limestone objects and artifacts.

The Folk Art Museum. In Agiou Andreou street stands, since 1985, the Folk Art Museum, housed in a neoclassical building, recently restored. Over 500 exhibits, ranging from the 19th to the 20th century, such as rural costumes, the loom, samples of Cypriot handicraft, embroideries, wedding crowns, etc are housed in six rooms.

The "**Dasoudi**" (copse) of Lemesos covers a relatively limited area, some 14 hectares, close to the Nautical Club. Since 1980, it hosts a modern organised beach of the Cyprus Tourism Organisation. A small area in the eastern part of the stretch has been built up, offering facilities such as restaurant, pub, cafeteria, refreshment stands, parking places and a number of sports facilities.

The **Municipal Gardens** host mediterranean, tropical and sub tropical plants, as well as trees normally found in oceanic climates. An open-air theatre hosts a variety of plays during the summer months. The busts of Lemesos' two great men, Christodoulos Sozos, patriot and hero of the 1912 wars and parliamentarian and mayor of Lemesos and Nikos Nikolaides, a great author, adorn the Gardens. The zoological corner, hosting a variety of animals, offers entertainment and scientific knowledge to the visitor. Directly opposite this corner, one can visit the Natural History Museum.

The *Wine Festival* is held, since 1961, in the Municipal Gardens of Lemesos, usually in September. A giant vine-producer dressed in the traditional costume, welcomes visitors at the entrance of the Gardens, while the motto remains constant: "Drink Wine to Live More". The festival lasts for a few days during which wine of all varieties is offered free of charge to the visitors. The kiosks of the main wineries exhibit their products inviting passers-by to test their wine. The Lemesos Wine Festival revives for a few days and on a small scale the ancient Dionysia and Linaea festivities. The ancient Greek festivities in honour of Dionysos, the God of vine and wine, were accompanied by common symposiums. These were organised free of charge by the State and included wine tasting, group dancings, songs, poetry and theatrical performances. Nowadays, hundreds of thousands of people, local and foreign of all ages, mingle together and under the influence of wine sing and spend unforgettable moments.

"Dasoudi", Lemesos

Top: The Wine Festival at the Municipal Gardens, Lemesos
Bottom left: Treading on the grapes to produce juice
Bottom right: Carnival parade at Lemesos

Lemesos is the town of Cyprus' *carnival,* a celebration recently introduced in other towns which have not yet attained the grandeur and splendour of Lemesos' carnival. It usually takes place in February or March, a week preceding Lent. It lasts for about 10 days, during which nightclubs, tavernas, hotels, clubs and discotheques provide evening entertainment in fancy costumes. There are numerous parties and dances during the last week, when everybody is disguised with masks and colourful fancy costumes. The parade is unique, with crowds thronging the streets to cheer the floats.

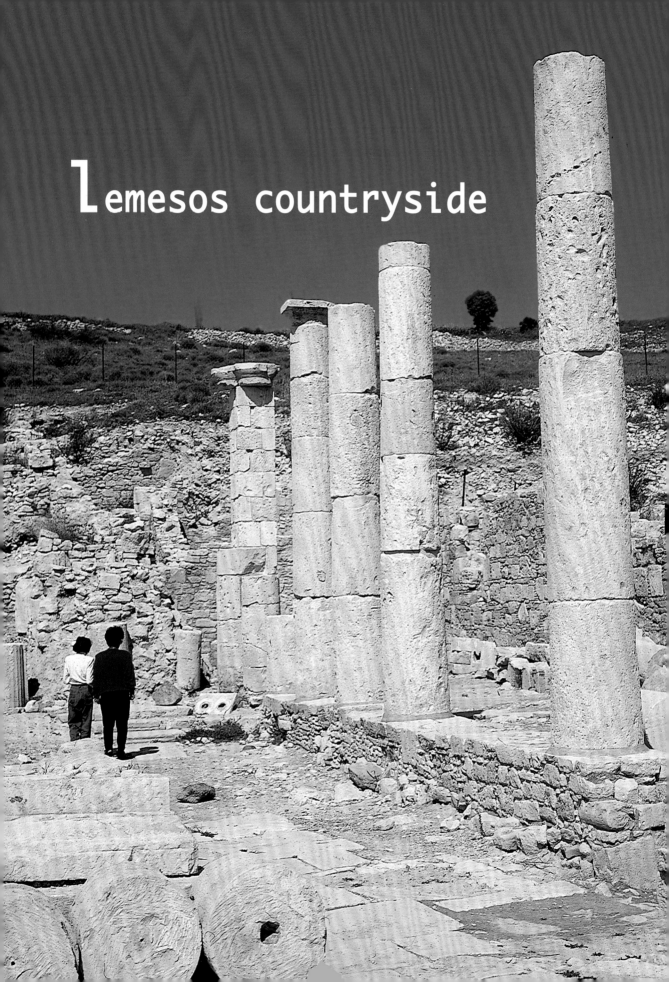

Lemesos countryside

Amathous, one of the ancient kingdoms of Cyprus, is now a vast area of ruins. It is not known exactly when Amathous was founded, though Amathous' local character is attributed through testimonies to 310 B.C. Amathous developed into a city early on and continued to flourish until the Byzantine years. The hill, which still dominates the environs, developed into a place of worship for Aphrodite, according to Catulus, or, a joint place of worship for Adonis and Aphrodite, according to Pausanias. It would appear that the Temple of Aphrodite, unearthed to a great extent by the archaeological spade, is quite old and was still in use during the 4th century A.D.

The *archaeological excavations* at the site focus on the Acropolis and the Temple of Aphrodite, on the supposed palace, the city walls, the ancient forum, the ancient harbour, the basilica and the two necropoles, east and west of the city. The Temple of Aphrodite dates back to the 1st century B.C. according to the experts and belongs to the Roman period. However, previous constructions have been unearthed. References mention this "site as the supposed palace of Amathous". Research as regards the presence of city walls has brought to light a series of successive fortifications, while, closer to the sea, a section of the walls and a Classical or Archaic tower has been incorporated into sizeable walls, dating back to the Hellenistic period. The western gates to the city have also been revealed. The excavations in the forum have brought to light columns, capitals, arcades, sewers, spacious yards, inscriptions, baths and cisterns. The ancient harbour of Amathous was probably built in the 4th century B.C., during the Ptolemaic period in Cyprus. It seems that the harbour was in use for only a short period. It soon silted up from the sediment carried down from the slopes of the Acropolis. To the east and west of Amathous one encounters the two necropoles, where hundreds of large and small graves, some looted, some intact, have been discovered. Most of the graves are carved out of the solid rock. Recent excavations concerning the walls of the city have disclosed the western gate by the sea, some additional towers and more details of the wall structure. In the 4th century A.D., Amathous became a Bishopric and it continued as such well into the Byzantine period. The huge growth of the city and the fame of its kingdom, not only in Cyprus but also in the then known world, may be the main reason for which Cyprus was called "Amathousia".

Left page: Amathous around ancient agora

Bottom: The Basilica of Amathous

Top: Kolossi stores

Right page: Kolossi tower

Kolossi Castle. The castle was most probably erected in the 14th century, though the middle of the 15th century is also mentioned as a probable date. What is certain is that the Knights of St. John arrived in Cyprus soon after the Latin occupation of Cyprus and in 1210 they were given the feud of Kolossi by King Hugh I. The Order, known as a Grand Commandery, owned vast properties in Cyprus, with Kolossi as the headquarters. The well known sweet wine of Cyprus (commandaria) got its name from the Grand Commandery of the Knights. At the beginning of the 16th century, with the consent of the Order, the area of Kolossi was transferred to the family of Cornaro, though with the conquest of Cyprus by the Turks the family lost its rights on this vast property. Internally the castle is divided into three storeys. The lowest floor with the arched roofs was used for storage purposes. The first floor consists of two large rooms, used as a kitchen and dining room. The entrance was defended by a drawbridge. To the right of this door is a large painting of the Crucifixion. The second floor also consists of two large rooms with two fireplaces, both of them decorated with the badge of Louis de Magnac. In these rooms lived the Grand Master of the castle. Next to the windows of this storey as well as of the first storey there are window seats. A circular staircase leads to the roof from where an extensive view can be enjoyed. Surrounding the castle were the houses of other noblemen as well as the vaulted barn of the knights. Close by are traces of the sugar mill where sugar cane was ground, while the aqueduct which supplied water for the working of the mill is still present, east of the castle.

Close to the imposing castle of Kolossi stands the **Chapel of Agios Efstathios.** The three-aisled chapel of the 15th century with its Byzantine architecture has some preserved frescoes. On the old iconostasis stand four portable icons, one of which portrays the Madonna, dating back to 1864.

Kourio mosaics

Episkopi, the successor settlement of ancient Kourio, stands on a rise with a fertile plain stretching to the south. In Episkopi there are a number of historical and archaeological sites such as the *settlement of Faneromeni* to the south-east, which belongs to the Middle Bronze Age, *Pamboula* settlement from the Early Bronze Age, the *necropolis of Kaloriziki* dating back to the 12th century B.C. and the *necropolis of Agios Ermogenis* to the south-west, which hosts a great number of tombs including the tomb of Saint Ermogenis. *Serai* or *Seragia* is the site south of Episkopi where relics of a medieval built-up complex lie. Two arched rooms, the relics of a church and a store house have been preserved. Most probably the church dates back to the 7th c. A.D. In the large store house hundreds of clay conical pots were found, used mainly for the processing of sugar. The **Museum of Kourio** at Episkopi, housed in a traditional two-storeyed building with a paved courtyard, originally destined as a private house of archaeologist McFadden, consists of two rooms. In the first room marble statues, tombstones, terra cottas, amphorae, decorated pottery, etc are exhibited. The second room exhibits findings from Faneromeni, Pamboula, the Sanctuary of Apollo and the tombs of present day Episkopi.

Of all the ancient kingdoms of Cyprus, **Kourio** is probably situated on the most conspicuous topographic position. It is built on a rise, about 60m high, with three steep, almost vertical, sides. Herodotus refers to the tradition that Kourio was founded by Greeks from Argos (Peloponnisos). It appears that during the Hellenistic and Roman periods Kourio was still an important centre, while during the 4th century A.D. it was destroyed by earthquakes. It was also seriously affected by the Arab raids of the 7th century A.D. After all these raids the bishopric of Kourio was transferred to Episkopi. The most interesting sites of the ancient city of Kourio are: *(A) The Theatre.* To the south of the complex an amphitheatrical natural hollow hosted a Roman theatre which had a capacity of about 3,500 spectators. The theatre was built at the end of the 2nd century A.D., was slightly restored in the 3rd century and was probably abandoned in the 4th century. The original theatre was used for perfor-

Kourio Theatre

mances of Greek tragedies and comedies. In recent years, it has been restored and is used for Greek tragedies and other performances. *(B) The House of Eustolios.* Next to the theatre are the remains of the House of Eustolios, consisting of thirty rooms with a bathing complex, dating from the 4th to the middle of the 7th century A.D. The floors of the porticoes are paved with beautiful mosaic compositions depicting fishes, birds and a partridge with Greek inscriptions. *(C)* The old-Christian *basilica of Kourio,* dating back to the 5th century A.D., is one of the most spacious basilicas of ancient Cyprus. The basilica was the cathedral of the first bishops of the town. The visitor can see the granite pillars which separated the aisles from the main body of the church. The basilica of Kourio was destroyed by the Arab raids of the 7th century A.D. and was replaced by the bishopric (episkopi) at the neighbouring village of Episkopi. *(D) The Roman Forum and the Nymphaeum* date from the early Hellenistic period to the 7th century A.D. The Roman forum is situated in the middle of the town of Kourio and was the meeting place of the citizens as well as the market-place. The Roman nympheum, built with huge hewn limestone blocks, was the central public space for water supply as well as the sacred building of Nymphae, the protector deities of the water. *(E) The House of Gladiators* obtained its name from the mosaic compositions representing gladiators, fighting in pairs. *(F) The House of Achilles,* most probably constructed in the 2nd century A.D., was a public place for the reception of officials. It is worth seeing the mosaics which depict Ulysses at Skyros where he recognized Achilles, disguised as a woman. The visitor should roam about the entire complex to look at the drainage system with the clay conduits, which served a town of about 30,000 people.

The Stadium of Kourio lies about 2km west of the archaeological site of Kourio. Built in the second century A.D., during the Roman era, it was used for some 200 years. It has a horseshoe periphery with three entrances, two in the long sides and one in the curved one. The dimensions of the stadium are 217m x 17m which correspond to the normal dimensions of almost all Graeco-roman stadia.

The Sanctuary of Apollo. Apollo, a significant deity of ancient religions, was considered to be the god of light, sun, poetry and music. At ancient Kourio Apollo was worshipped as the god of forests from which he obtained the name of Apollo Ilatis (in ancient Greek Hyle=forest, woodland). The Sanctuary of Apollo was used from the 7th c. B.C. until the 4th c. A.D. Starting the exploration from the western door of the site (Pafos gate) the visitor can see on the left the broad steps leading to two narrow elongated chambers, which most probably housed the visitors. Visitors, however, were housed in the southern building situated near the arcade. Five chambers separated by a corridor were either used as dormitories or for the display of offerings. No doubt the people's offerings were numerous. In a pit north-east of the southern building, hundreds of pots and statues were found, dating from the 5th century B.C. to the Roman era. From the votive pit a narrow paved street leads to the temple of Apollo. The four-pillared temple was small because ceremonies were usually carried out in the open. The reconstruction of the temple began in 1979. Coming back from the temple, on the left, stood the ancient temple. Northwest of the baths, next to the priest's residence, lies the Archaic Precinct (Temenos). The wrestling place (palaistra) where athletes exercised in an open courtyard, surrounded by a row of columns, lies to the south-east of the complex.

Left: Temple of Apollo
Bottom: Palaistra, Sanctuary of Apollo Ilatis
Right page: Kourio Basilica (5th c. A.D.)

Pissouri dominates the surrounding area. The tall, large stores by the coast, now in ruins and the traces of an old pier witness the commerce of carobs in recent years. Pissouri beach, which is quite large, is protected by cape Aspro. Hotels, restaurants and tourist apartments have appeared recently at this beach.

Laneia, south of Trimiklini, is a village with a rich traditional architecture. At Laneia there are narrow, winding cobbled streets, elongated two-storeyed houses with tiled roofs, wooden carved doors and windows, courtyards with flowered gardens and large wine jars. The church of Panagia (B.V.M.), dating back to the late nineteenth century, is situated at the centre of the village. In the apse is preserved an early 16th century icon of B.V.M.

Sotira is a very old settlement with two significant churches, that of Agios Georgios, now restored, and that of the Transfiguration, both of the 17th century. Visitors to Sotira will most probably concentrate their interest and attention on the archaeological site of the neolithic settlement of Sotira (4500-3900 B.C.). The houses are irregular, circular or ellipsoidal, very close to each other, separated only by very narrow corridors. The foundations are built with stone, while the upper part was most probably made of baked bricks, reeds or even wood covered with mud. It is not yet known how the settlement was destroyed, though the numerous earthquakes of those times might explain its abandonment.

Pissouri beach

Traditional architecture, Laneia

Lofou is a settlement dating back to at least medieval times. It was granted by the King of Cyprus, James I, to his brother Janot de Lusignan in the 14th century. The houses of Lofou are unique in traditional architecture. The cobbled streets are narrow and winding with large wine jars still lying close to the entrance of the houses. However, the main feature of the village are the cisterns. As many as 73 cisterns existed in the village. It was a laborious job to transport water on donkeys from the river, which lay at a relatively big distance, so people constructed cisterns in front of their houses in the courtyard. The winter rain was collected in these stores, while the water on the tiled roofs also ended up in the

cisterns. The church of B.V.M. Evangelismos is a 19th century building standing on a higher elevation than the rest of the houses. Some paintings are probably recent. About 1.5 km outside the village is the chapel of Profitis Ilias. The chapel preserves an unusual icon which, according to tradition, has the power to prevent rain, especially in early summer when storms could ruin the corn lying in the threshing floors.

Visitors to **Koilani** can see an interesting traditional architecture. On the north-west of Koilani, the hill *Afamis,* 1,153m high, is a conspicuous landmark. The hill gave its name to a popular wine of Cyprus. Two

Top: Lofou village
Right: Fresco from Agia Mavra, Koilani

museums in the village embody the long history of the village, namely the Ecclesiastical Museum and the Vine Museum. In the Ecclesiastical Museum treasures such as old ecclesiastical books, old gospels, portable icons, altars, consecrated vessels, etc, date back from the 13th century to recent times. The museum was built in 1987 close to the church of Panagia. The Vine Museum, housed in a traditional building, exhibits agricultural tools, particularly those connected with vine-growing. **Agia Mavra church,** about two miles from the village, is a fifteenth century building with a narthex that was added later. The church, originally a monastery, is famous for its history, its frescoes, the holy well and a plane-tree close by, which Sakellarios considers as the "biggest plane-tree of Cyprus". The paintings, most of which belong to the 17th century, look worn though the frescoes of Agia Mavra and Agios Timotheos (16th century), the Pantokrator, a few prelates and saints, scenes from the Old and New Testament and paintings from the life of Christ are still preserved.

Top: Agros village
Left: Gathering roses at Agros
Right page: Traditional architecture, Omodos village

Omodos is a wine-producing village, famous for the Omodos wine press, known as *"linos",* one of the most renowned wine presses in the island. The history of the Monastery of the Holy Cross of Omodos is long and dates back to 327 A.D. when Agia Eleni visited the island. During the second decade of the 19th century, the Monastery was completely restored. The Monastery has a number of museums, such as the Museum of Byzantine Icons, the Museum of Local Art and the Museum of National Struggle 1955-1959.

The village of **Agros** is at a height of 1,150 metres above sea level. It is blessed with important places of historical and cultural interest as well as a fascinating natural environment, with intriguing flora and fauna and several nature trails. Traditional customs are maintained and the pretty, rustic houses are typical of the attractive mountain village style. According to the writer N. Klerides, the village owes its name to a monastery known as monastery of Megas (Great) Agros which pre-dates the present settlement. The church of the monastery stood until 1894 when it war replaced by the present-day church of Panagia Eleousa. Many icons, the iconostasis and the altar of the Monastery of the Great Agros were saved and later placed in the church of Agia Eleousa. Another church Agios Ioannis of Prodromos, built in 1760, without frescoes but with an interesting architecture, attracts the attention of visitors.

Mesapotamos falls

Left page:
Top: Psilo Dentro, Platres
Bottom: "Linos" wine press at Omodos

Pano Platres has been christened the king of Cyprus' mountainous resorts. Kings and governors, enterpreneurs and millionaires, eminent writers and artists have been hosted in its hotels. Seferis, the noble laureate, impressed by the environment of Platres, wrote the following verse in his poem Eleni. *"The Nightingales won't let you sleep in Platres".* The visitor to Platres should not neglect to visit *Psilo Dentro* and sit for a few moments under the shade of the plane and walnut trees. A few visits to neighbouring sites of interest, such as Kalidonia Falls, Mesapotamos and Arkolachania, are recommended.

Arkolachania, *a picnic site,* can be visited via Kato Amiantos, Saittas, Moniatis or Platres. Close by are the **Mesapotamos falls,** which could be called double rapids. The waters drop first onto one platform and then onto a second. Close by is also the old monastery of Mesapotamos, founded in the 12th century.

Kalidonia falls, 3.5 km north of Platres, have a height of 12 metres, and all the characteristics of real falls. The rapids drop very abruptly because they meet resistant gabbro rocks that have not yet been eroded.

Troodos is the central mountain range of Cyprus, with Olympos (Chionistra), its highest peak (1,951m), visible from all parts of Cyprus. Very often the snow on Troodos is heavy, enough to break the branches and tender tips of the pine-trees. According to tradition, on the peak of Olympos stood a temple of Venus (Aphrodite), while according to another tradition in early Christian times there stood, close to the Olympos peak, various churches; their remnants are no longer traceable. Skiing at Troodos is a favourite sport. Locals and foreigners can enjoy a few nature trails at Troodos during the four seasons of the year.

Trooditissa Monastery, with its height of about 1,300 metres a.s.l., is considered to be the loftiest monastery of Cyprus. What is fascinating about the monastery is its rich history and tradition. One could seek the history of the monastery in an isolated cave, close to the monastery. According to tradition, a monk carrying the icon of the Madonna, a painting by Apostle Luke, left his native country and reached Akrotiri, close to the monastery of Agios Nikolaos of the Cats, around 762 A.D. Having spent about 25 years at the monastery of Agios Nikolaos, one day, guided by a bright star, he arrived at the present monastery of Trooditissa. He lived in a cave, known as the "Cave of Trooditissa", until he died. After his death, the candle in the cave, continued to be lit by shepherds, hunters and lumbermen. It is this candle and the icon of Panagia that prompted people to build the monastery in about 990 A.D. Though the history of the monastery between 990 and 1570 A.D. is obscure, Trooditissa was looted and destroyed in the 16th century, like most monasteries in Cyprus. In 1585 the church was burnt but the monks managed to save the divine icon of Panagia. A new single-aisled church, painted entirely, was subsequently built. In 1842 the church was again burnt, though it was restored one year later. The church is now three-aisled, while the iconostasis is new. Between 1954 and 1974 the monastery was restored by increasing the cells and the rooms that can host guests. Many miracles are attributed to the icon of the Madonna. Childless women visit and pray for a child. A pair of buckles still lies near the icon and women who wish for a child must wear them to have their wish granted.

Right: Trooditissa monastery
Left page: Snow-covered Troodos

pafos town

Neoclassical buildings housing primary and secondary schools

According to tradition, Pafos was founded by Agapinor, a hero of the Trojan war from Arkadia. During the Hellenistic and Roman periods, Pafos was the capital of the island. In 15 B.C., the city was razed by an earthquake, but was rebuilt with the help of Emperor Octavian Augustus. It is in Pafos that apostles Paul and Varnavas preached Christianity in 45 A.D.

During the Byzantine period Pafos ceased to be the capital of Cyprus, being replaced by Salamis. During this period Pafos was subjected to numerous attacks and raids by the Arabs, especially in the 7th century A.D. The Pafos fort, aimed primarily at repelling Arab raids, was built during this period. During the Frankish period, the Pafos port was used as a stop for east-west traffic, while the Pafos fort was still considered quite strong. During the Venetian period the Pafos fort was not only abandoned, but was also destroyed so as not to fall into Turkish hands. During the Ottoman occupancy of Cyprus, Pafos, along with the rest of the island, fell into decline; many visitors described it as "a deserted city".

During the Colonial period, which began in 1878, Pafos was recognised as the capital of one of six districts.

In the years following Independence and until the Turkish invasion (1974), Pafos continued to be a relatively small town of Cyprus offering limited services and attracting few tourists and visitors. However, after 1974, Pafos enjoyed an unprecedented tourist activity following the construction of numerous hotels. Tourist-related industries (restaurants, souvenir shops, night clubs, etc) have also enjoyed significant growth. Pafos is currently an administrative, mini-industrial, commercial, tourist, educational, cultural and entertainment centre.

Pafos

N

"Tombs of the Kings" Rock-cut tombs

ARISTARCHOU
ARION
ANANIA
GIALOUSAS

GEORGIOU CHRISTOFOROU
ARIADNIS ZININONOS
ANDREA NIKOLAOU
ANDREA CHRISTODOULOU
GALATIAS ZININONOS

Agios Kendeas
ARCHIEPISKOPOU MAKARIOU II
MITROPOLITOU NIKODIMOU MYLONA
NIKOU ANTONIADI
Municipal Library
ERMOU
GRIVA DIGENI

GLADSTONOS
Agios Ioannis

IVIS MM
IVIS MM
KALLIOTOU
AIGANNOU
IAKOV IAKOVIDI
GALATOPOULOU
25 MARTIOU 2
Town Hall
Municipal Gardens

VYRONA
RODOTOU

MICHAIL KYPRIANOU

KATO PERIVOLION

ANAPAFSEOS

Byzantine Museum
Agios Theodoros
Bishopric
ELEFTHERYSIS
MARIAS LOIZIDOU
Ethnographic Museum

VASILISSIS VERENIKIS
PYRAMOU
KONSTANTINOU KAVAFI

TAFON TON VASILEON

AMFITRIONOS

STRATI MYRIVILI
LORENTZOU MAVILI

AGIAS THEKLIS
G.MICHAIL
ILEKTRAS
G.SAVVA
ALES ATHINAS
TEGEAS
ILYSION
EKANSI
CHRYSANTHEMON
Agios Epifanios

ADAMANTIOU KORAI
IAKOVOU CHRISTODOULIDI
DIMITRIOU GEORGIOU
FRYNIS
NIOVIS
PINELOPIS
APOSTOLOU PAVLOU
AGAPINOROS

PANTELI MICHANIKOU
PAPARRIGOPOULOU
CH.FILIPPIDI
TH.ZINONOS
CHRISTOU ARISTODIMOU
PANDORAS
ALEXANDREIAS
PRIAMOU
ANDROMACHIS
LEFKADOS
EDESSIS
PTOLEMAIDOS
ATLANTIDOS

AIANTOS
TILEMACHOU
GEORGIOU SEFERI
ANGELOU SIKELIANOU
ANDREA KARKANITSA
MICHAIL NIKOLAOU
KIRKIS
IRAS
ALAMANAS
DRAMAS
GLYFADAS

EKTOROS
AGINOROS
Cyprus Handicraft Centre
AVLONAS

TILEMACHOU
PARI
PELAPAISIOU
AGISILAOU
AIOLOU
P. PASCHALIDI

ELEFTHERIOU CHANDRINOU
IFAISTOU
KADMOU
ANTIGONIS
AGIOU AMVROSIOU
PENTADAKTYLOU
DANTOU
DIMITRIOU KONSTANTINOU
PRIAMOU

TAFON TON VASILEON
PARMENIONOS
PROMITHEOS
Rock of Digenis
AGION ANARGYRON
AGIOU MAMANTOS
AGIOU ILARIONOS
OROUS
AG. FILONOS

Walls (north-west gate)
Garrison's camp
Fabrica
AGIOU LAMPRIANOU
Agios Lamprianos
Agios Agapitikos
AGION ANARGYRON

Agia Solomoni
Theatre
AGIOU ILARIONOS
AGIOU GAVRIIL
PLOUTARCHOU
AGIAS SOLOMONIS
ONISILOU
AGIOU AGAPITIKOU
Agia Marina
AGAPINOROS

(Probable acropolis)
Agora
Odeion
Asklepieion

AGIAS GALATIANIS
Latin Cathedral
SARANTA KOLONON
Agia Faneromeni
IKAROU
Agios Georgios

AGIAS KYRIAKIS
IFIGENEIAS
AGIAS FANEROMENIS
KONSTANTIAS
DEFKALIONOS
LAMPOUSIS
MESAORIAS
AGIOU GAVRIIL

Archaeological Park
MINOOS
PAFIAS
AGAS ANDRONIKOS
Frankish Baths
Agios Georgios
TEFKROU

House of Dionysus (Mosaics)
AREOS
AFRODITIS
Chrysopolitissa Basilica
AGIAS NAPAS
KLYTAIMNISTRAS
Agios Antonios
APOLLONOS
NESTOROS

House of Aion (Mosaics)
Saranta Kolones
STILIS AGIOU PAVLOU
St Paul's Column
AGIOU ANTONIOU
APOLLONOS

House of Orfeus (Mosaics)
KYRIAKOU NIKOLAOU
Agia Kyriaki
THEOSKEPASTIS
APOSPOU
IASONOS
KIKERONOS

House of Theseus (Mosaics)
Theoskepasti
ARTEMIDOS
DIAGOROU

Limeniotissa Basilica (Ruins)
Customs Office
LIDAS
ALKMINIS
Aquarium
DIONYSIOU
APOSTOLOU PAVLOU
STASANDROU
POSEIDONOS
Municipal Beach
MELINAS MERKOURI
OTHELLOU
POSEIDONOS

Harbour
KATO PAFOS
Fort

0   250 metres
1:11 000

© SELAS Ltd

The Odeion of Pafos

Archaeological sites and cultural monuments

The **basilica of Chrysopolitissa**, originally built in the 4th century A.D. with significant modifications made until the 7th century A.D., when it was destroyed by the Arab raids, was one of the largest in Cyprus. The floor of the basilica was covered with colourful mosaics, some of which are preserved.

The **Odeion** dating back to the 1st century A.D. was most probably roofed, and was used for musical contests, public orations and plays. It was most probably destroyed by the earthquake of the 4th century A.D.

The **Asklepieion**, the healing centre and temple of Asklepios, the mythological God of medicine and healing, is a building complex with many rooms dating from the 2nd c. A.D.

St Paul's Column. St Paul together with St Barnabas and Ioannis Marcou journeyed in 45 A.D. from Salamina to Pafos, which was the seat of the Roman governor, Sergius Paulus. The convincing preaching of Paul converted Sergius Paulus to Christianity. Legend says that St Paul, before the conversion of Sergius Paulus, was given 39 lashes (saranta para mia) by the Jews. The column where St Paul was tied and lashed by the Jews is known as "column of St Paul". This, however, is not recorded by the Acts.

The **Sanctuary of Apollo Ilatis** constituted a place of worship of one of the deities of ancient Greece. Apollo was regarded as the God of sea, shepherds, medicine, music, song and spiritual life as well as the protector of health and happiness. The sanctuary dates back to the 4th century B.C., when Pafos was founded.

The **Agora** or market-place which dates to the 2nd c. A.D. consists of a colonnaded square courtyard

71

Left page:
Top: The Asklepieion
Bottom: Basilica of Chrysopolitissa

Top left: The Sanctuary of Apollo Ilatis
Top right: The Theatre
Bottom left: The column of St Paul
Bottom right: The Basilica of Panagia Limeniotissa

measuring 95 x 95 metres. Visitors can see the surviving Corinthian columns and capitals, as well as the steps leading to the stoa and the shops.

The **basilica of Panagia Limeniotissa**, dating back to the 5th century A.D., is close to the restaurants of the harbour. The basilica, destroyed by an earthquake in the 12th century, is mentioned by St. Neofytos. Visitors can observe the size of the three-aisled building, the colourful mosaics as well as a few restored columns. The basilica is dedicated to "Virgin Mary of the Harbour".

The **Tombs of the Kings** or the Palaiokastra (Old Castles), lie to the north-west of ancient Pafos. The site was the necropolis (cemetery) of Pafos with hundreds of underground rock-hewn tombs. Though there is no known connection with kings, it is possible that eminent Ptolemies, living in Pafos, might have been buried in the tombs. Crosses and some mural paintings indicate that in early Christian times the tombs acted as a refuge for Christians. The tombs which date back to the 3rd century B.C., are reached by steps and have open peristyle courts surrounded by burial chambers.

Left page:
Top: The Tombs of the Kings
Bottom: The harbour of Pafos

Top left: The Frankish baths
Top right: Relics of the Cathedral of the Latins
Bottom left: The catacomb of Agia Solomoni
Bottom right: The cave of Agios Agapitikos

The **harbour** of Pafos is currently full of colourful fishing boats and yachts, the latter hailing mainly from mainland Europe. In the past, pilgrims arrived here in numbers before proceeding to the temple of Aphrodite at Kouklia. Cafes, restaurants and tavernas around the harbour cater for a large number of visitors.

The **Fabrica Hill**. According to Loizos Philippou, Fabrica Hill was named as such because, during the Middle Ages, there stood at the site a textile mill. It probably dates back to Hellenistic times. It was used during Byzantine times and was quarried in later years.

The **cave of Agios Agapitikos** lies in the north-eastern corner of the Fabrica Hill. According to tradition, those in love should visit the cave unobserved, leave some coins and take some earth from the cave which they should place into their desired one's drink.

The **Theatre** dates back to the end of the 4th c. B.C. or beginning of the 3rd c. B.C. It had a diameter of 80 m and it could accommodate 8,000 spectators. It was most probably the biggest theatre in Cyprus.

The **Frankish Baths.** A well-preserved Frankish building dating back to the Lusignan period (1192-1489 A.D.). The baths, which currently retain their original appearance, could accommodate approximately one hundred bathers.

The **Catacomb of Agia Solomoni.** Visitors have to descend twenty or so steps to find themselves in front of four subterranean chambers, a holy well and an open courtyard. At a later stage the largest chamber was

The castle of Pafos

transformed into a church which was originally frescoed; traces of the frescoes can still be seen today.

The **Cathedral of the Latins (Panagia Galatariotissa).** The ruins of a Frankish cathedral, possibly of the 14th c., is known by the locals as the Madonna of "Galatariotissa" (Virgin Mary of the Milk). The church was restored by Francesco Cantarini, the Latin Bishop of Pafos.

The **Fort of Pafos** was, according to an inscription above the main entrance, "built by Ahmed Pasha in 1592 A.D.". It is a reconstruction built on the ruins of a previously existing Frankish fort. According to other historians and writers, the fort dates even further back

to the Byzantine era. History and the geographical isolation of Pafos required the construction of a fort next to the harbour. During the Ottoman period, some of its rooms were used as prison cells while the British used the building as a storage area for salt.

Saranta Kolones. This Byzantine fort of Pafos was most probably built during the third quarter of the 7th century A.D., in order to offer protection to the harbour during the Arab incursions. The name Saranta Kolones (Forty Columns) derives from the large number of granite columns strewn across the archaeological site. Today, the visitor can see a square fort surrounded by external walls and a moat. The fort collapsed during the 1222 A.D. earthquakes.

Saranta Kolones (Byzantine fort of Pafos)

Pafos Mosaics

(a) The house of Dionysus. The House of Dionysus was built on the foundations of an earlier Roman house, this having been built on the foundations of a building belonging to the Hellenistic period (325-50 B.C.). The most important rooms to be seen are: *The Room of Narcissus, The Room of Four Seasons, The Room of the Peacock, etc.* The name "House of Dionysus" is mainly due to the many representations of Dionysus, the god of wine.

Most probably the House of Dionysus was destroyed by the earthquake of the 4th century A.D. Since then the mosaics had remained covered until they were restored recently.

(b) The House of Theseus. The mosaics of the villa of Theseus date back to the 2nd century A.D. Two mosaics depicting mythological representations are worth seeing: *Theseus killing the Minotaur* and *Achilles' birth.*

(c) The House of Aion. The mosaics of the House of Aion date back to the 4th century A.D. Five mythological scenes are worth observing: *The Bath of Dionysus, Leda and the Swan, Beauty contest between Cassiopia and the Nereids, Apollo and Marsyas, Triumphant procession of Dionysus.*

(d) The House of Orpheus. The mosaics of the House of Orpheus belong to the 3rd century A.D. Three mythological scenes are particularly worth seeing: *Orpheus and his Lyre, Hercules and the Lion of Nemea, The Amazon.*

(e) The House of the Four Seasons was named as such because the broken mosaic floor represents the personification of the four seasons. The Mosaics belong to the first half of the 3rd century A.D.

ΘΙCΒΗ

ΠΥΡΑΜΟC

ΙΚΑΡΙΟC

ΟΙΠΡΩΤΟΙ
ΟΙΝΟΝΠΙΟΝ

Museums

Ethnographic Museum of Pafos. This is a private ethnographic museum, until 1971 known as Folk Art Museum. The visitor can see costumes, particularly rural costumes and trimmings, traditional carved wooden furniture, farming tools, kitchen utensils, clay artefacts, looms, woven articles, etc.

Archaeological Museum. The museum exhibits a vast number of archaeological findings. Visitors can examine exhibits from the Neolithic, Chalcolithic and Bronze ages, the Iron Age and Classical period, the Hellenistic and Roman periods, the early Christian periods and the Byzantine and Middle Ages.

Byzantine Museum. The extremely interesting Byzantine Museum of Pafos lies within the precincts of the Pafos Bishopric. It houses a great number of Byzantine icons, dating mainly from the 12th to the 19th century, collected from churches and monasteries of the district of Pafos. The Byzantine Museum contains also liturgical books, firmans, manuscripts, woodcarvings, crosses, silver reliquaries, priests' uniforms, etc.

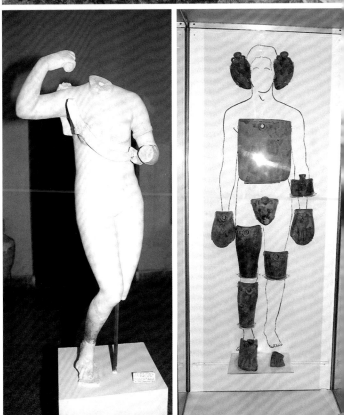

Top: From the Ethnographic Museum of Pafos
Centre: Virgin Odigitria, 16th c. From the Bishopric of Pafos
Bottom: Armoured Aphrodite and Hot water bottles for each member of the body (From the Archaeological Museum of Pafos)

Left page: Pafos Mosaics
Top: Thisbe and Pyramus, 3rd c. A.D.
Bottom: Icarius and "the first who drink wine", 3rd c. A.D.
(Photos, courtesy of the Dept. of Antiquities)

Churches

Panagia Theoskepasti. The church is built on a protruding rock, close to the sea, east of Chrysopolitissa basilica. As it stood on such a conspicuous rock, it could be easily discerned by invading Arabs during their raids. However, according to a legend, the church of the God-protected Holy Virgin Mary was veiled with dark clouds and rendered invisible as soon as the Saracens approached it. When once a Saracen managed to enter the church and tried to steal the golden candle, divine power cut off his hands. The present-day church of Panagia Theoskepasti was restored on the old foundations in 1928, preserving its Byzantine architectural style. It is believed that the miraculous silver-covered icon is one of the seventy (icons) painted by the Evangelist Luke.

Church of Agia Kyriaki . The three-aisled church of Agia Kyriaki, built in the 11th-12th century A.D., lies in the north-eastern corner of Chrysopolitissa basilica. Originally constructed by the Latins, and later transformed into a Greek Orthodox church, particularly after the conquest of Cyprus by the Turks, it acquired a low belfry in 1906. Though not painted today, nevertheless some traces of painting indicate that the church might have been entirely covered with paintings. The large icon of Agia Kyriaki lies on the right corner in front of the iconostasis.

Left: Panagia Theoskepasti church
Bottom: Church of Agia Kyriaki

Pafos countryside

Encleistra of Agios Neofytos

Agios Neofytos Monastery. Agios Neofytos was born in 1134 at the village of Kato Drys. Since the age of 17, he lived in the monastery of Agios Chrysostomos, on the Kyrenia range, as a lay-brother, cultivating the vineyards. He believed in ascetic life and soon left the monastery to travel to the Holy Land. He returned to Cyprus and, while wandering in the coastal plain of Pafos, came across a rocky surface with a cave in the present locality of the monastery. The topography, the solitude and the presence of a spring were considered ideal for his future ascetic life. At the age of 25, he carved his Encleistra (cave) and made it habitable. The cave currently preserves a narthex, the main body of the church, the sanctum and the cell of Agios Neofytos. The paintings of the Encleistra were undertaken by Theodoros Apsevdis. At the age of 65 he carved the

Left: St George isle (Pegeia)
Right: Five-domed church of Agia Paraskevi, Geroskipou

Right page:
Top: Coral Bay
Bottom: Sea caves (Pegeia)

"Upper Encleistra", above the main cave, where he could withdraw and escape from the ever-increasing visits. He died at the age of 85. About 200 years later the main church of the present monastery was built. The Saint's relics are currently preserved in this 15th-century church. Though the church is devoted to Theotokos Maria, it is known as the church of Agios Neofytos.

Coral Bay is a horse-shoe cove with its edges ending in abrupt cliffs, while in the middle an extensive fine-grained sandy beach is bordered by the rock of coral limestone. On the northern edge of the cove, which is a tiny peninsula with cliffs on three sides, the ancient settlement of *Maa-Palaiokastro* has been unearthed, which dates back to the 13th century B.C. Achaean settlers, after the decline of Mycenean centres in Peloponnisos (Morea), arrived in Cyprus, mainly attracted by its copper mines. They chose this strategic position to build their fortified settlement, which was, however, soon abandoned, most probably in the first decades of 1200 B.C.

Kantarkastoi Caves or Pegeia Sea Caves. An earthen road on the Pafos-Agios Georgios road, about 2km south of Agios Georgios church (Cape Drepano), leads to the most spectacular sea caves of Cyprus, known as Kantarkastoi caves or sea caves of Pegeia. Cracks and

joints in the strata of the chalky rocks encouraged the waves to open caves which now constitute labyrinthine formations. Just opposite, in the sea, lies the picturesque isle of Agios Georgios, at a distance of about 300 metres.

Geroskipou. According to tradition, implied even by the name of the village (translation: Holy Gardens), here, or slightly west of the settlement, were the holy gardens of the Goddess Aphrodite. Pilgrims from Nea Pafos passed through Geroskipou before reaching the temple of Aphrodite at Kouklia (Palaepafos). Since 1978 Geroskipou boasts a Folk Art Museum with displays of the Cypriot civilization, particularly of the last two centuries. The Museum hosts costumes, agricultural tools, house utensils, wood carvings, etc. Besides, the village is the home of the famous tasty Geroskipou turkish delights, displayed on stalls on both sides of the road. The industry was established in the 19th century. The five-domed Byzantine *church of Agia Paraskevi* was built somewhere in the middle of present-day Geroskipou. Built in cruciform style, it dates back to the 11th century. The visitor should spend some time to examine the frescoes of Byzantine art. The best preserved paintings are the Nativity of Christ, the Baptism, the Crucifixion, the Resurrection of Lazaros, The Last Supper, Christ Washing, Judas Betraying Christ, Christ before Pilate, etc.

Petra tou Romiou (Rock of Romios) is probably the number one place of interest in Pafos. The rock is loaded with myth, tradition and memories. The fruitful Greek imagination, chose, out of all Greek islands, Cyprus as the birth place of the Goddess of Love and Beauty. It is surprising that geologically there is no relation between the rock and the adjacent rock formations. This partly explains the tradition that the Rock was thrown there by the Byzantine hero Digenis Akritas. It is from the white foam of the waves that Aphrodite (Venus) said to have been born. As she emerged from the foam, the gold-dressed Horae received her with joy. They placed on her head a beautiful gold crown. Finally she came to rest at Kouklia (Palaepafos) where her temple, now ruined, is found.

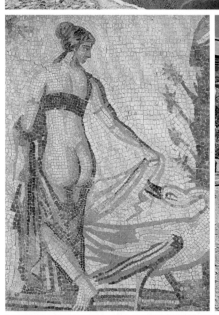

Top: The Lusignan manor house, Kouklia

Left page:
Top: Pierced stones, part of a very old olive press (Kouklia)
Centre left: Leda and the Swan
Centre right: Relics from the Sanctuary of Aphrodite, Kouklia
Bottom left: Clay bath, Kouklia
(From the Archaeological Museum of Kouklia)
Bottom right: Conical stone serving as a cult idol in the Sanctuary of Aphrodite

Kouklia (Palaepafos). The modern settlement itself stands on the ruins of Old Pafos (Palaepafos). Here lies the famous grand temple of the Goddess of Love and Beauty, which served people for hundreds of years until the advent of Christianity. Visitors can focus their attention on the following: *(i) The Temple of Palaepafos.* The area around present-day Kouklia has been inhabited continuously since the 15th century B.C. The worship of Aphrodite, the dynasty of Kinyrades, and the "Afrodisia" ceremonies impress and attract visitors to the village. The ruins in their present condition stretch south of the settlement up to the Chateau of the Lusignans. The huge hewn blocks of stone, the thick walls, the large courtyards and the mosaics are very impressive. The original features of the temple were, however, altered significantly by later Roman changes and additions, as earthquakes made extensive repairs necessary. The Afrodisia festivities, which consisted of musical, poetic and athletic contests and sacrifices to the goddess, were an annual event and lasted for four days. Pilgrims gathered at Geroskipou and Achni and from there they headed together for the shrine. The Goddess Aphrodite was associated with life, love and fertility. *(ii) The Lusignan Manor House.* This is a 13th c. A.D. building, used as the manor house of the Lusignans, who established sugar-cane plantations in the fertile land between the sea and the present-day settlement. *(iii) The Museum.* In the chambers of the Manor House the visitor can observe rich samples of ceramics, inscriptions in Cyprosyllabic script on marble, limestone, capitals, swords, mosaics, statuettes, clay lamps, clay idols. *(iv) The church of Katholiki* is a medieval building which served the Latin community. It dates back to the 12th century, though its western section was restored in the 16th century. Currently, the church is long and single-aisled with a dome. The visitor can observe traces of the 16th century paintings. *(v) Encleistra.* About 3.5 km north of the settlement, at the base of a deep valley, there is a rock-hewn cave, known as encleistra. A few frescoes are preserved in the cave.

Top: Central Square of Polis

Right page:
Top: Western Chrysochou beach
Bottom: Baths of Aphrodite

Polis. This small "ancient town" was built thousands of years ago. Today it is called Polis, in the Hellenistic and medieval times it was called Arsinoe and in ancient times it was known as Mario. Today it is engaged in tourism, offering its almost unlimited sandy and pebbled beaches to the holiday makers. Archaeological excavations near the town's hospital have unearthed a 6th-century basilica. Opposite the hospital and a few metres to the right, remains of the Hellenistic period were discovered, while a few metres further east a 5th c. B.C. temple has been found. Historians mention that *Mario* was conquered in 449 B.C. by Kimon. Ptolemy demolished and destroyed the town. Thus, on the foundations of ancient Mario, Arsinoe was later created, named after the sister of Ptolemy Philadelfos. With Christianity spreading in Cyprus, Arsinoe acquired a bishopric; during Frankish times, the seat of the Pafos bishopric was transferred here.

The central square of Polis with cafés, restaurants and souvenir shops attracts tourists.

Latsi. The picturesque harbour of Latsi has a horseshoe shape, with two small lighthouses with a wooden pier about 45 metres long towards the centre. The beach to the west of the harbour has become a sought-after swimming area.

The road from Latsi comes to an end at the **Baths of Aphrodite.** Though not an extensive sandy beach, quite a few people do swim in the clear waters. The coastline is rocky with lush vegetation. A path leads from the tourist pavillion to the Baths of Aphrodite amid dense vegetation. At the base of the limestone, on the fissures of the rock grow fig trees, their broad-leaved branches giving abundant shadow. The semi-circular pool has a depth of about half a metre and a perimeter of about five metres. According to tradition, Aphrodite, Goddess of Love took her bath here.

Top: Rocky coastal cliff east of Akamas
Right: Serapias vomeracea

Left page: View of Akamas

Akamas is an area of natural beauty, with impressive flora and fauna, mainly attributable to the undisturbed nature of the region and the diversified scenery (rock faces, gorges, spring valleys, water courses...). An impressive number of plant species are found here such as pines, junipers, wild olive and carob trees, lentiscs, rockrose asphodels, thyme, the Cyprus tulip, cyclamens and particularly a unique strawberry tree (Arbutus unedo) which, so far, has been located only in Akamas. The fauna is also impressive and consists of a large number of bird species, mammals, reptiles and butterfly species.

Left page: View to Fontana Amorosa

Top: A unique view of the eastern Akamas coastline
Bottom: View close to the Baths of Aphrodite

Top: Sand dunes fringing Ammoudi beach

Right page: Avakas Gorge

Ammoudi. Following the western road from Agios Georgios (Pegeia) visitors encounter a large fine-grained sandy beach known as Ammoudi. This lovely beach has a length of about 400m and a width of 30m. The sand dunes reach a height of about 15m, supported by lentisks of an umbrella-shape. The most impressive aspect of the beach, however, is the **Turtle Hatchery,** established in 1978. Turtles coming from the west arrive at this isolated beach to lay their eggs, mainly in August-September, before they carry on their journey. At the same time turtle eggs from other beaches of Cyprus are transported here to be hatched in safe conditions. The makeshift hatchery functions only during the summer months.

The Avakas Gorge. The Avakas river starts in Arodes village and ends at Toxeftra. If visitors wish to explore the two-kilometre gorge, walking is recommended from Arodes village. If visitors wish to see the mouth of the gorge only, the visit can be accomplished from Toxeftra, near the sea.

Exploring the gorge from Arodes village, the visitor can walk along the deep, steep-sided valley with cliffs on both sides, at some points as high as 100m. Huge rocks, fallen from the sides, block the valley. The flora and fauna of the area is very rich and unique.

Table cloth made by Fyti weavers

Fyti, with its traditional architecture, particularly the well-carved limestone blocks used for the building of elongated rooms and two-storeyed houses, fascinates the visitor. It is weaving, however, that is the speciality of Fyti. In past decades nearly every household kept a "voufa", (loom), while until 30 years ago there were as many as 40 weavers; currently there are only a few. Women at Fyti weave curtains, handkerchiefs, pillow-cases, bed covers, napkins, table-cloths and a number of other products. The visitor can always find a souvenir to buy.

Chrysorrogiatissa Monastery

Agia Moni Monastery

Chrysorrogiatissa Monastery, about 800 metres a.s.l., is situated west of Pafos forest. The monastery was founded in 1152 A.D. by Monk Ignatios who found at Moulia (Pafos) the miraculous icon of Panagia, believed to have been painted by St Luke the Evangelist. Ignatios took the icon to the mountain where the monastery is now built. Barsky, a Russian monk who visited the monastery in the 18th century, describes it as "poor, but located on a picturesque site". At the end of the 18th century the monastery was restored, with the single-aisled church being built on the foundations of the older one. The church in the middle of the monasterial complex impresses with the frescoes above the three entrances. The icon of Panagia Chrysorrogiatissa, with the exception of the face of Virgin Mary, has been silver and gold-covered since the 18th century.

Agia Moni. Between Chrysorrogiatissa monastery and the new, planned settlement of Statos-Agios Fotios, stands the historic monastery of Agia Moni. According to tradition, the monastery was built by St Eftychios and St Nikolaos in the 4th century A.D., on the ruins of the temple of Hera. In the 12th century the monastery possessed a workshop of manuscript-copying, while during the Frankish period it possessed three annexes. It was during the Turkish occupation of Cyprus that it declined and became an annex of Kykko monastery. In 1820, the monastery was abandoned. The entrance to the restored monastery is through an arched door with an inscription on the left side, noting that the monastery was restored in 1696.

Left page: Road between Panagia and Cedar Valley

Top: Moufflon, living mainly in the forest of Pafos

Stavros Tis Psokas. Stavros tis Psokas is a forest settlement, with tiled, steep pitched houses made of wood. In an enclosure of this forest settlement the visitor can see the moufflon, the national animal of Cyprus. Though in the past moufflons could be encountered in the Troodos forest, currently they are confined mainly to the forest of Pafos. Moufflon is as old as the first inhabitants of Cyprus or the first neolithic settlements of the island. In neolithic times it was hunted and caught for its meat as well as for its bones. Later on, particularly in the Hellenistic-Roman times, its presence is testified to by the mosaics of Pafos. In the Middle Ages it was the game of the noble Frankish ruling class. In 1939, the forest of Pafos, where the animals live, was declared a game reserve area. The moufflon belongs to the sheep family, with the male having horns like those of a ram and the female bearing no horns. The animals live from 15 to 20 years, are very elegant and powerful. As soon as they feel the presence of man they disappear. Normally, they appear in groups of five or six.

Larnaka town

Top: Ancient Kitium (with remains of city walls)
Right: Limestone statue of Zeus Keravnios (Kitium), 5th c. B.C.
(Photo, courtesy of the Dept of Antiquities)

Left page: Foinikoudes Promenade

Larnaka, the successor city of Kitium, one of the ancient kingdoms of Cyprus, developed in the same geographical environs as Kitium. Kitium, according to archaeological and historical evidence, was settled by the Phoenicians during the 9th century B.C. The founding, however, of the city can be traced back to the Mycenean era. Kitium was a Phoenician city between the 9th century B.C. and 312 B.C., at which time it was conquered by the Ptolemies. It would seem that the Phoenician temple of Astarte was built during the first few years of the Phoenician advent in Cyprus. The advances of Alexander the Great against the Persians, the later alliance of the Cypriot kingdoms with Antigonus or Ptolemy and the submission of Kitium to the latter, an event which led to the killing of the king of Kitium, brought about the termination of Phoenicocracy in the city. It is during this period, in 334 B.C., that Zenon of Kitium, the well-known Stoic philosopher and greatest thinker of ancient Cyprus,

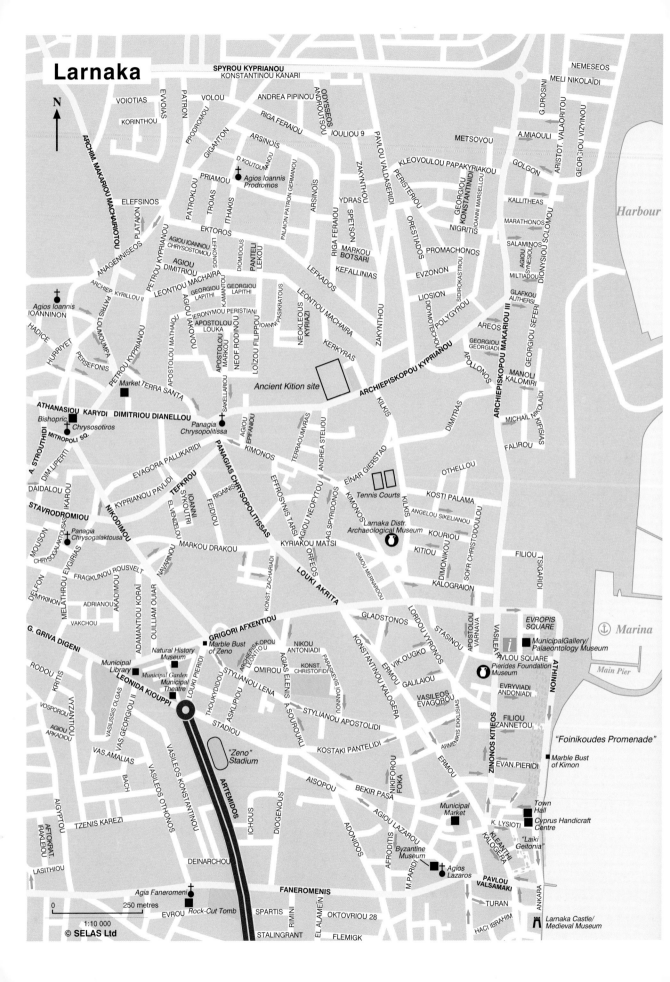

Kalavasos archaeological site

was born at Kitium. An important event, of the 1st century A.D. is Larnaka's acceptance of Christianity. According to tradition, the first bishop was Saint Lazarus, who settled in the city following his resurrection by Jesus. The city kept the name of Kitium during Byzantine times. In the 4th century A.D., however, Kitium, along with other cities of Cyprus, suffered catastrophic damages due to earthquakes, while the calamitous Arab raids between the 7th and the 10th centuries A.D. had serious repercussions on the city. During the Frankish and Venetian periods, the city of Zenon, was known as "Alykes" or "Salines", probably because of the lakes and the salt warehouses in the area. During the Frankish period, as well as the short Venetian period, the salt from the neighbouring lake brought a substantial income and was one of the main exports of the island. It may have been during this period, though it has not yet been fully ascertained, that "Alykes" also took on the name of "Skala", originally probably from a French word pertaining to a landing or mooring spot. During the Venetian period, nothing of note occurred in Larnaka, mostly because the Venetians were more interested in the utilisation of the resources that Cyprus and Larnaka had to offer than the progress and welfare of the city. As a consequence, in 1570 the armies of Lala Mustafa conquered Larnaka unhindered; and the conquest of the entire island followed shortly after that. In spite of the fact that the Turkish rule was accompanied by an administrative system geared towards misery, humiliation and arbitrary decisions, it differed from the previous regimes due to the cosmopolitan nature of the city, especially the presence therein of dozens of consulates, as well as

Europeans. It is possible that the name "Larnaka" was given to the city during the initial stages of Turkish rule, probably due to the discovery of a large number of sarcophagi (in greek "larnakes") which came to light with the rife activities of many grave-robbers. Excavations, though, started during the Venetian years and it is possible that the name "Larnaka" was first used during the 15th century. British rule started in July 1878 and the most important occurence of this period was the dissolution of the consulates in Larnaka and their transfer to Nicosia. The value of Larnaka as a commercial port diminished due to the increased competition from the ports of Famagusta and Limassol. Larnaka is currently an administrative, industrial, commercial, tourist and education centre. The town also hosts many sports events and is the seat of the Kitium Bishopric.

Ancient Kitium. Ancient Kitium lies beneath the buildings of present-day Larnaka. The largest area excavated, to the north of Larnaka, known as Area II, permits a glimpse into an important part of the history of ancient Kitium. The earliest relics date back to the 13th century B.C. The reconstructive work carried out on a broad scale by the Achaeans during the 12th century B.C., however, contributed to the creation of the most impressive architectural remains seen today. It was during this period that the original walls were replaced by cyclopean walls, made up of two rows of monoliths. The main temple of this period is quite large (35 x 22 metres) and is considered the most important temple revealed at Kitium. The other important period of the history of Kitium started with the arrival of the Phoenicians in Cyprus who came mainly for commercial reasons in the 9th century B.C. The abundant copper deposits of Cyprus and its plentiful lumber also led the Phoenicians to this area of the island. The large temple was turned into a place of worship for Astarte, which was destroyed by fire. It was rebuilt later on and, during the 7th century, it was renovated and divided into three chambers. The temple was destroyed once again by fire in 312 B.C., around the time of the demise of the Phoenician dynasty.

Hala Sultan Tekke. The entire building complex of Tekke, comprising the mosque and the minaret, the rooms, the fountains and the gardens, are in the midst of date palms and cypress trees. Up close, the carved stone of the monument, its cobbled paths, the delicately chiselled stone cornices around the entrances and the Arabic inscriptions, are impressive.

Kamares Aqueduct

Hala Sultan Tekke

Opposite the entrance to the mosque one notices an octagonal structure containing eight water outlets, where pilgrims wash their feet before entering the mosque. The most significant component of Tekke is the grave of Um Haram. The tomb is connected with the first Arab raid in Cyprus, carried out by Moab in 649 A.D. Um Haram took part in this expedition. Upon arrival of Moab's fleet to Cyprus, a mule was given to Um Haram, on which she was to ride to the interior of the island. En route, she fell from the animal and was killed, being buried at that very spot. To some, Um Haram was the Prophet Mohammed's aunt, but recent research carried out by followers of Islam, proved that Um Haram was the aunt of Anas Ibn Malik, secretary and loyal servant to the Prophet. The site took its present form in 1816. Tekke continues to be among the three most important Muslim religious sites after the Ka'aba in Mecca and the Shrine of Mohammed in Medina.

Kamares Aqueduct. When during the 18th century Larnaka suffered from a shortage of water, Bekir Pasha, the Ottoman governor of Cyprus at the time, constructed an aqueduct stretching from the Tremithos river, through the area north of today's Kiti dam, and reaching the city of Zenon. The construction of the Larnaka aqueduct began in 1747 and was completed three years later, in 1750. The hewn limestone with which the aqueduct's arches were built, were brought from the ancient settlement of Kitium. Today, the traveller passing by Kamares is impressed by the 33 arches still standing, each one of a different width.

The Marble Bust of Zenon is close to the Municipal Gardens. Zenon, was born in 334 B.C. and moved to Athens to follow the teachings of Crates, Stilbo, Xenocrates, Pelemon and Diodorus Cronus of Megara. Since these philosophers belonged to different

Church of Agios Lazaros

schools of thought, it was only natural that Zenon should acquire a broadly based philosophical expertise. It seems that the Cypriot philosopher was influenced by Crates, Stilbo and Heraclitus, since his teachings reveal elements taken from all three: Crates' cynicism, Stilbo's stalwartness and Heraclitus' austerity. At the age of about 40, he formed his own philosophical school in the Pikili Stoa which, because of its seat, became known as Stoicism. The reputation of the new philosopher soon attracted pupils from all over Greece. Zenon lived a patient, sparse and modest life. His self-control was an example for imitation during classical times. As regards "blabbermouths", the Cypriot philosopher used to say: *"Nature has given us one tongue and two ears, so that we may hear twice as much as we say".*

The Bust of Kimon. The Greeks, the Athenians in particular, fought hard and long for the liberation of Cyprus from the Persian yoke. The culmination, however, of the relationship which Cyprus enjoyed with the Athenians was the death of Kimon, the great general, who, together with Anaxicrates left Athens in 450 B.C. in order to free Cyprus from the Persians. Having liberated the city of Marion, Kimon proceeded to Salamis and Kitium. At Kitium, however, either as a result of injury or sickness, he died, whereupon his comrades decided to keep the news of his demise secret. Albeit, upon leaving the island, the Greeks were granted a double victory at Salamis, with the Phoenician fleet in the sea and the Persian armies on the land. It was this victory that gave rise to the well-known phrase, with reference to Kimon: "Even in death he vanquished". The people of Larnaka, as proof of their love and adoration to the great general, erected a marble bust in his honour in 1927.

The church of Agios Lazaros. Agios Lazaros, the beloved friend of Christ, was forced, after his miraculous resurrection, to seek shelter at Kitium, now Larnaka. According to tradition, he became the first bishop of Kitium and the first church dedicated to him was built to serve the needs of the small population of Kitium at the time. The reconstruction of the church was undertaken by the emperor of Byzantium, Leon VI the Wise, around 890 A.D. He sent money as well as skilled workmen to build the Byzantine church we can see today, with the agreement to receive the relics of St. Lazarus, which had been found in a marble sarcophagus in the original church. The actual church was subsequently extended and renovated. In older days the church functioned as a monastery as well. The gilted iconostasis, an 18th century work, is a masterpiece of art. An icon which demands particular attention is that of Agios Lazaros, work of 1738.

Larnaka Fort, next to the well-known "Foinikoudes", was built, according to some writers, by the Turks in 1625. It seems, however, that it existed during the Venetians and was put to different uses following the Turkish occupation of Cyprus. The Fort of Larnaka has undergone many changes and modifications by the Turks, the British and the Cypriot Government. Its shape is square, with extremely thick walls, especially towards the sea. One can still see the few battlements, similar to those found on other Venetian forts. The

Larnaka Fort

The Marina of Larnaka

spaces which were later turned into prison cells are on the ground floor. An external staircase leads to the roof of the initial fort, where one can ascertain the thickness of the walls. Furthermore, huge earthen pots and stone anchors, discovered at Tekke and ancient Kitium, can be seen in the fort.

The Archaeological Museum. In the limited space of the Museum there are treasures from the entire Larnaka district. In one of the rooms are hosted findings, especially pottery, of the neolithic age, the bronze age as well as of the geometric, archaic, classical, Hellenistic, Roman, early Christian periods and very few specimens of the Middle Ages. The early bronze age (2500-1900 B.C.), the middle bronze age (1900-1650 B.C.) and the late bronze age (1650-1050 B.C.) are well represented. Besides, the faience, ivory and alabaster objects, all imported, bear indisputable witness to the commerce and the international relations between Cyprus and different foreign countries. The second large room of the museum houses mainly statues, tombstones and inscriptions made of limestone and marble.

The Pierides Museum. A spacious, two-storeyed building at Zinonos Kitieos street, built in colonial style, houses the Pierides Museum. The archaeological collection was started by Dimitris Pierides, head of the family, in 1939. The prestige of the Pierides family, contributed to the arrival in Cyprus of a Swedish expedition between 1927 and 1931. Gustave Adolph the 6th, King of Sweden and personal friend of the Pierides family, participated in the expedition. Exhibits from the neolithic settlement of Choirokoitia, impressive red pottery of various shapes from the bronze age, specimens representative of the Mycenean period, earthenware statues of the Hellenistic and archaic periods, pottery of the Hellenistic Roman and Byzantine periods, etc. are exhibited.

The Natural History Museum has been founded in the small public garden of Larnaka. In small rooms are exhibited embalmed birds of Cyprus, endemic as well as migratory, reptiles and colourful butterflies. Rather more representative is the collection of rocks and fossils originating from different regions of Cyprus. In an open space very close to the small rooms of the museum the visitors can see ducks, chickens, parrots and especially a moufflon, an animal unique in the Pafos forest.

The Marina of Larnaka, close to the palm trees of the town, hosting around two hundred crafts of all types, has been in operation since 1976. The colourful crafts with their upright masts, the platforms, the piers, the impressive breakwater as well as other auxiliary constructions, constitute a special and picturesque corner of Larnaka.

Foinikoudes (Date Palms).
For decades the Foinikoudes (date palms) along the seafront of Larnaka, particularly between the marina and the fort, constitute the trade mark of Larnaka.

The Larnaka Salt Lake. If you visit the Salt Lake in the summer you will usually find it all dried up, with an enormous layer of salt covering its bottom. In the old days part of the salt production used to be exported to other countries. If you visit in winter, the picture is entirely different. The lake is filled with water in which colours, shadows and shapes are reflected. Different kinds of migratory birds, especially ducks and flamingoes, arrive from the cold countries of the North and embellish, with their colour and presence, this beautiful and unique wetland.

Makenzey Beach. Visitors can find here many coffee shops, restaurants, tavernas and small hotels, all close to or on the beach. Makenzey beach, obtained its name from a British man called Makenzey, the first to have built, just after the second world war, a small restaurant in the area.

Makenzey beach

Larnaka countryside

Top: Royal chapel of Agia Aikaterina
Left: Pyla Tower

Pyla, in the north of Larnaka bay, is the only village in the free part of Cyprus where Greek and Turkish-Cypriots live together. Pyla's roots are extremely ancient, since archaeological excavations have proved that the area used to be densely populated during the Late Bronze Age. *Pyla tower,* a medieval building, which acted as an observatory has remained intact, even if the floor and the roofs of this three-storeyed building have not survived.

Pyrga. Between Kornos and Psevdas, in a shallow valley, lies the village of Pyrga. The *royal chapel of Agia Aikaterina*, one of the most interesting relics of the Kingdom of Lusignans, is situated in the west end of the settlement, on a hummock. It was built, in Gothic style, at the beginning of the 15th century. It has a rectangular shape, three doors and a vaulted roof. It is built with igneous rocks of reddish or greenish colour, which have been collected from the adjacent area. The interior of the chapel was originally painted, like most Byzantine churches. It was later abandoned for a long time and looted by the Mamelukes, after the defeat of Ianos at Choirokoitia in 1426. Only few frescoes were saved. However, some paintings remain.

Hagiography in Cyprus

Stavrovouni. Following a steep road at the summit of the mountain is the monastery of Stavrovouni, built around 327 A.D. The full story of the founding of the church, according to tradition, is as follows: During her return from a pilgrimage to the Holy Lands, Agia Eleni, mother to Constantine the Great, brought a piece of the Holy Cross. A storm forced her ship to drop anchor at Mari. Exhausted by the storm, she fell asleep in the royal tent where, in her sleep, an Angel of the Lord appeared and said: *"Most respected Queen, the Lord has sent me to inform you of His will. In the same way that you have built churches in Jerusalem, so shall you build in Cyprus, where you shall place a piece of the Holy Cross".* Agia Eleni awoke frightened. She sought the pieces of the Holy Cross and discovered that they were missing. She searched for them everywhere, but

in vain. Suddenly, a servant turned her attention to a distant mountain (today's Stavrovouni), whose apex was veiled in a golden-red glow. Servants were sent to the spot, where they discovered the pieces of the Holy Cross. Agia Eleni then knelt and prayed and ordered that a church dedicated to the Holy Cross be erected at the top of the mountain. The chapel of Agioi Konstantinos and Eleni initially served as a secret crypt where monks took shelter during raids. The monastery is renowned for the piece of the Holy Cross it contains. The church was fully rebuilt in 1426, following the battle of Choirokoitia, at which time the Egyptian general looted and razed the church. In 1888, the monastery was completely destroyed by fire. The only artifact that remained intact was the piece of the Holy Cross. The church of Stavrovouni has been painted by Kallinikos, one of the leading painters of ecclesiastical frescoes. *Women are not allowed to enter the Stavrovouni monastery.*

Choirokoitia Neolithic Settlement
On the slope of a hill, archaeologists have unearthed the neolithic settlement of Choirokoitia, which dates back to the 7th millenium B.C. Since 1936 when archaeological excavations commenced, Choirokoitia has become well-known for its circular houses, its stone-built defensive wall and its narrow corridors. The local stone and the pebbles carried by the river were used abundantly, while the first inhabitants of the neolithic settlement knew very well how to cultivate the land and tame wild animals. In addition, they were engaged in hunting and fishing. This very ancient community was well organized and highly developed. Their burial customs exhibit respect to the dead. On the stone foundations of the circular house, most probably baked bricks were added, while on top of the roof, branches and leaves of trees were spread. Certainly, the hard igneous rocks which the river carried down on its bed from the mountains, were worked on to produce tools, such as flour mills, axes, etc. Close to the bank of the river, a reproduction of five neolithic dwellings allow the visitor to study, in detail, the circular houses of the Neolithic Period. The neolithic settlement of Choirokoitia has recently been included in the world heritage list of monuments.

A small medieval church dedicated to Panagia tou Kampou (B.V.M. of the Plain) was most probably built by the Templars. It is a single-aisled, domed church, built with hewn limestone blocks.

Bottom left: Choirokoitia neolithic settlement
Bottom right: Stone bowl from Choirokoitia
(Photo, courtesy of the Dept. of Antiquities)

Left page: Stavrovouni Monastery

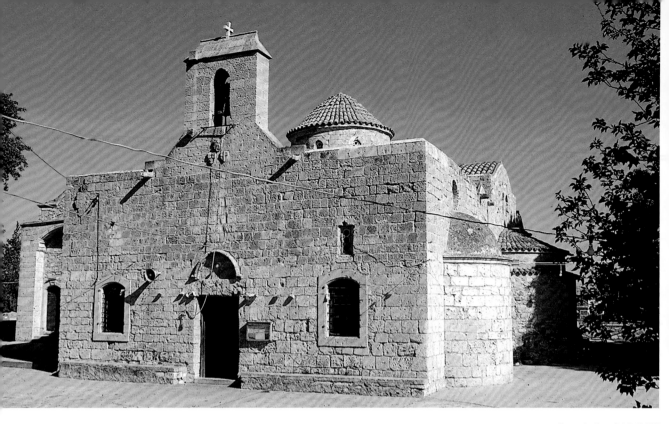

Panagia Angeloktisti, Kiti

Venetian tower (Perivolia)

Panagia Angeloktisti at Kiti. Northwest of Kiti, on a very gentle rise, stands the Byzantine Church of *Panagia (Madonna) Angeloktisti* (the Angel-built). According to tradition, it was built by Angels, who at midnight descended from the Heavens and built the church. South of the church a Frankish chapel of the 14th century which once belonged to the medieval family of Gibelet has been added. On the north side of the church a small dark chapel has been added, which, according to Jeffery, was a small mortuary chapel. The main church is three-aisled, built in the 11th century, on the foundations of an older Byzantine basilica. Dim traces of frescoes on the walls witness that most probably the church was originally entirely painted. However, the most glorious item to be seen in the church is the mosaic in the central apse, which shows the Madonna holding a Child. She stands between the Archangels Michail and Gabriel.

The Tower of Perivolia is situated on an imposing hummock, about 500 metres from the sea, very near the cape and the lighthouse. The only opening is a rectangular window in the northern part, over which there is a Venetian coat of arms. A ladder is needed in order to enter the tower, similar to the ladder used in Venetian times when the tower was in operation. The building, eight meters high, consists of two storeys separated by a wooden floor. It seems that the guards spent most of their time on the upper floor. Most probably the first floor was used for storage or for other needs.

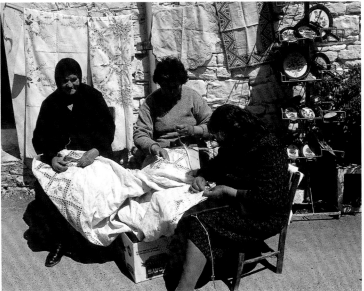

Top: Pano Lefkara village
Bottom left: Embroiderers at K. Lefkara
Bottom right: Lace-making at Lefkara

Pano Lefkara village fascinates visitors with its meandering narrow streets, the wooden doors and windows, its balconies, the horizontal layers of the local limestone building material as well as all other details of traditional architecture. The principal church dedicated to the Holy Cross is a large building of the mid-nineteenth century which replaced a Byzantine church. According to tradition, the church was built by Agia Eleni and it contains a fragment of the True Cross. The rich gilt iconostasis, dates from the 18th century. The laces are a speciality of women, whose husbands travelled, in the past, all over the world to sell them. Leonardo da Vinci, when he visited Cyprus in 1481, purchased lace made at Lefkara for the Milan Cathedral. Most of the embroidery is sold locally to tourists who visit the village specifically for the purchase of lace.

Ammochostos (free part)

Ammochostos (Famagusta) district lies in the eastern part of Cyprus, comprising nine settlements in the free part of Cyprus, the rest lying in the occupied part of the island. Within this part of the Ammochostos district lies a major tourist centre, namely Agia Napa-Protaras, which attracts nearly one quarter of the island's tourists. The capital of the district is currently Paralimni with a population of 7.749 inhabitants.

The free part of Ammochostos, known by the name of Kokkinochoria *(Red villages),* is an area where agriculture, industry and tourism co-exist. The main agricultural product is the *potato.* Besides the numerous boreholes drilled in the area and the prolific use of windmills, a very conspicuous feature in the landscape of Paralimni, irrigation has recently been improved by the Southern Conveyor Project, conveying water to the area from other districts of Cyprus.

Agia Napa, before 1970, was a small village not as rich agriculturally as the rest of the Kokkinochoria villages. Today, with its fine-grained white sandy beaches and its luxurious hotels, it has become the centre of an international tourist area with an international reputation. Agia Napa, featured profusely in Venetian maps, appears to have been known before the advent of the Venetians in Cyprus, during which time the monastery was built. According to information imparted by Cesnola, the monastery was possibly built during the Lusignan period, while the large expanses of the aqueduct, which conveyed water to the monastery, are possibly of Roman origin. Corinthian capitals unearthed in this old settlement seem to give testimony to the fact that Agia Napa was inhabited as far back as ancient times or that it was an outgrowth of another ancient settlement in the surrounding area.

Agia Napa's little harbour is in essence a fishing shelter. The colourful boats, the fish taverns and its restaurants constitute an impressive picture.

Nissi Beach. The small isle from which the beach has obtained its name constitutes a challenge for exploration. Currents and waves exploit the weaknesses of the rock and continuously undermine it. They wear away the isle and the little points, but simultaneously add to the width of the beach, even setting up a wall. This little wall, which connects the beach with the isle (known as tombolo) is a peculiarity of the area.

Caves and arches. The rock formations, right next to the white sands of the beach, are very interesting. To the east of Agia Napa one comes across the largest caves and grandest coastal archways of Cyprus.

Left page: Windmills, a characteristic feature of Paralimni

Bottom: Gathering potatos

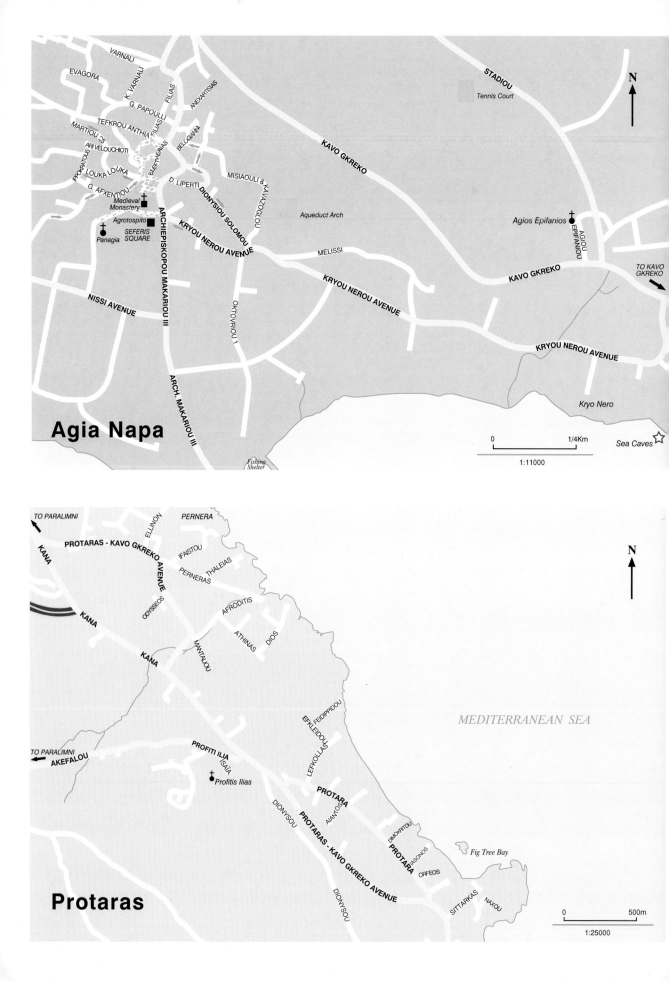

Agia Napa

VARNALI
EVAGORA
K. VARNALI
G. PAPOULLI
FILIAS
ANEXARTISIAS
TEFKROU ANTHIA
MARTIOU 25
FILIAS
ILIAS
ELEFTHERIAS
BELGRANM
ARI VELOUCHIOTI
PROKRATOUS
LOUKA LOUKA
G. AFXENTIOU
ELEFTHERIAS
D. LIPERTI
MISIAOULI & KAVAZOGLOU
DIONYSIOU SOLOMOU
Medieval Monastery
Agrotospito
Panagia
SEFERIS SQUARE
ARCHIEPISKOPOU MAKARIOU III
KRYOU NEROU AVENUE
NISSI AVENUE
OKTOVRIOU 1
ARCH. MAKARIOU III
Fishing Shelter
STADIOU
Tennis Court
KAVO GKREKO
Aqueduct Arch
Agios Epifanios
AGIOU EPIFANIOU
KAVO GKREKO
TO KAVO GKREKO
MELISSI
KRYOU NEROU AVENUE
KRYOU NEROU AVENUE
Kryo Nero

N

0   1/4Km
1:11000
Sea Caves ☆

Protaras

TO PARALIMNI
ELLINON
PERNERA
PROTARAS - KAVO GKREKO AVENUE
IFAISTOU
KANA
PERNERAS
THALEIAS
ODYSSEOS
KANA
AFRODITIS
KANA
ATHINAS
DIOS
MANTALIOU
TO PARALIMNI
AKEFALOU
PROFITI ILIA
ISAIA
Profitis Ilias
EPIKLEIDIPPIDOU
LEFKOLLAS
PROTARA
DIONYSOU
PROTARAS - KAVO GKREKO AVENUE
AIANTOS
PROTARA
DIMOKRITOU
IASONOS
ORFEOS
Fig Tree Bay
DIONYSOU
SITTARKAS
NAXOU

MEDITERRANEAN SEA

N

0   500m
1:25000

Top: Fishing shelter of Agia Napa
Bottom: Fisherman at work

Nissi Beach

NISSI BAY SNACK-BAR

Agia Napa Monastery. Undoubtedly, the monastery of Agia Napa is the most imposing cultural monument and the most interesting site of the settlement. The coat of arms over the main entrance and other details are indicative of the Venetian architectural character of the monastery. According to local tradition, however, its founding is based on the location of a cave which today forms the Orthodox chapel of the monastery. It was here that the icon of the Virgin Mary was discovered and the cave thus turned into a site of worship for the locals. At a later stage, this became known to the daughter of a noble Venetian family living in Famagusta. The maiden, distressed that her parents would not give their consent to her marriage to a commoner, abandoned her home and found retreat at this very place where she built a chapel, monastic cells, a flour mill and an olive press. Initially the monastery was inhabited by nuns and the chapel, as expected, was of a Roman Catholic order. Today, the edifice, symbol of the Roman Catholic denomination of the Venetian conquerors of the area, is next to the cave housing the Greek Orthodox chapel. Visitors to the Roman Catholic church can see worn frescoes. Another interesting feature within the confines of the monastery is the **aqueduct,** used to convey water from the north-east of the village. An outlet in the shape of a boar's head, found in the north side of the courtyard, may even date back to the Roman times. The most interesting feature of the courtyard, however, is the **fountain,** which includes an octagonal basin adorned with sculpured figures in bas-relief.

Marine Life Museum. The Marine Life Museum of Agia Napa, at 26 Agia Mavri Str, Agia Napa Municipality, is the first of its kind in Cyprus, housing shells and other specimens of Cyprus' marine life. The museum exhibits shells from the unoccupied part of Cyprus, turtles which periodically visit Cyprus and birds endemic to the island, as well as marine migratory birds.

Right: Fountain within the monastery complex
Bottom: Inside Agia Napa monastery

Left page:
Top: Sea caves at Agia Napa
Bottom: Tourists enjoy the unspoilt coastline at Konnos area

Pernera

A narrow coastal plain stretching about 5 km northwest of Gkreko to the east of Paralimni, has been given the name **"Protaras"**, a name well-known among international tourist circles. The true Protaras is, quite possibly, the site of ancient Lefkolla, which today is the small cove with the fine-grained sand and the little island, which the British have christened *"Fig Tree Bay"*. Wave-kissed coasts with jagged promontories and sandy bays, little isles and isolated rocks, sea caves and arches formed by the waves, a few scattered irrigated plots of fruit trees and vegetables, thousands of windmills; all these make up Protaras. Sprouting day by day on this natural scene are hotels, tourist apartments, souvenir shops, supermarkets, restaurants and many other tourist-related establishments. Lying on the warm beach of Protaras, gazing at the isle across the water, visitors from abroad know little about the ancient town of Lefkolla, the city-port that Strabo

mentions, where Cesnola discovered artifacts of Greco-roman origins. This locality is indeed very ancient. A series of little islands adorn the coast of Protaras, known to the locals as *"Nissia"*. Recent excavations at Nissia revealed 28 houses and a wall. Pottery, stone instruments and horns of deer have been found. The settlement is considered to be neolithic.

The isolated *chapel of **Profitis Ilias,*** built in carved reddish limestone, lies on a solidary outcrop dominating the area. The church we see today was rebuilt in 1984, on the foundations of an old church, which had almost been in ruins. Small, elegant and with no extra frills, following the byzantine rhythm of architecture, with plates built into the walls, it contains a tiny iconostasis with icons drawing their subjects from the life of Christ. The view from the outcrop is truly unique.

Paralimni: One can visit Paralimni by following the picturesque coastal road connecting Agia Napa, Gkreko and Protaras. It is a route full of contrasts, beauty, colour and tourist activity. There is, however, an alternative, shorter route via Xylofagou and Agia Napa. Paralimni (translated in English, "by the lake"), obviously obtained its name from the neighbouring *lake*. It is a large hollow where water collects only in winter months. Within the *municipality* of Paralimni side by side with the modern buildings, one can still see a number of traditional homes. Paralimni has not only grown in population and as a tourist centre but also in terms of commerce, the economy, education, re-creation and administration. In the centre of the municipality one can still see the farmers enjoying their coffee, talking among themselves and acting in ways which betray their agricultural background, reminiscent of years gone by. Of special interest within the village are three churches. The contemporary *church of Agios Georgios* is exceptionally large and three-aisled. The church is built according to the byzantine rhythm and has a walnut iconostasis. Next to the present-day church of Agios Georgios is an older church, dedicated to the same saint, dating back to the last century. In contrast to the contemporary church, this one does not contain many frescoes. There is, however, a gilted iconostasis with images in bas-relief, as well as several portable icons also dating back to the last century. The *church of Panagia (the Madonna)* appears to have been built with two chambers, even though it is obvious that the southern one was a later addition. Some residents mention an original, very old church, dedicated to Agia Anna and dating back to the 13th century. Built of local limestone rock, it used to be totally frescoed. Today the church is adorned with enshrined colourful plates. The carved iconostasis belongs to the 17th century.

Deryneia. One can admire in Deryneia the local architecture with the traditional homes and their impressive entranceways, supported by thin columns. Of all the churches strewn within the administrative boundaries of the village, the visitor should distinguish two: The *church of Panagia (the Virgin)* is old, built in Byzantine rhythm, though not belonging to that era. The *church of Agios Georgios,* which is probably older than the church of the Virgin, cruciform and domed, probably of Byzantine origin, contains worn frescoes. The church was originally completely covered with frescoes, even though today one can only see the fresco of Agios Georgios and a few others.

Ammochostos, as seen from Deryneia

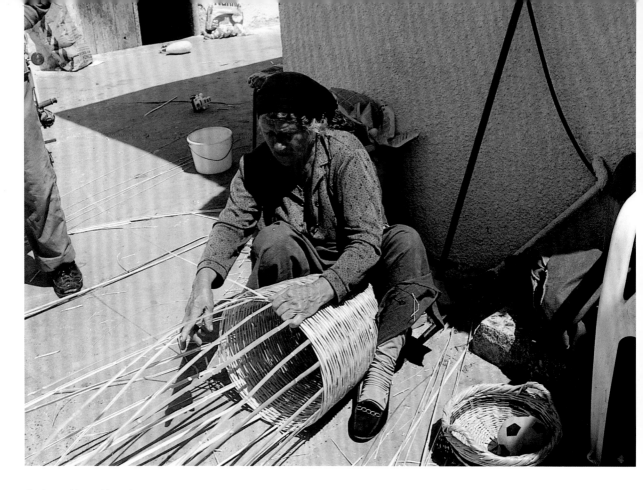

Basket-making at Liopetri

Sotira, a large agricultural village of the Kokkinochoria region, stands west of Paralimni lake. Apart from its rich traditional architecture, it is known for its cultural heritage, particularly its medieval and contemporary churches. The *church of Metamorfosis* (Transfiguration of the Saviour), three-aisled with an impressive iconostasis and capitals at the entrance, lies within the settlement. The old, domed, 16th century church of the Saviour, was initially larger. The *church of Agios Mamas,* cruciform and domed, an elegant little building dating back to the 15th century, still contains a few worn frescoes. The *church of Agios Georgios Chordakion,* outside and just west of Sotira, is also cruciform and domed. It was built in the 12th century, while a narthex, in the shape of a cross and possessing a dome, was added on to it. In this way, two domed churches joined internally, constitute an architectural building of beauty and an attractive monument. *The church of Panagia Chordakiotissa,* probably also dating back to the 12th century, is small, cruciform and domed with two niches in its interior left and right of the entrance.

Liopetri with traditional buildings side by side with modern ones, lies 14 km north-west of Agia Napa. The village is well-known for the art of *basketweaving*. The focus of village life is the central village square where one finds the village coffee shops and the medieval church of Panagia Eleousa (Virgin Mary). The medieval, domed *church of Panagia Eleousa,* built in Byzantine rhythm, impresses with its gilted iconostasis, its portable icons belonging to the last century, the fresco of the Virgin of Mercy on the north wall and of Saint Mamas on the south. The 15th century *chapel of Agios Andronikos,* built in cruciform Byzantine rhythm, today containing but a few worn paintings, was, at one time, entirely frescoed. Another stop that is a "must" for the visitor of Liopetri is the *"Barn of Liopetri".* It was in this barn that three youths made their final stand on September 2nd, 1958 and etched a glorious page of heroism in the history of Cyprus. At this spot, one of the most heroic episodes involving Cypriots struggling for their independence, took place.

Frenaros, lying in the centre of the Kokkinochoria region, comprises some fascinating traditional houses with spacious yards and arched entranceways. The village is very old, as a neolithic settlement (7500 B.C.) has been unearthed in its administrative limits. Its churches are many and interesting. The contemporary *church of Archangelos Michail* of a Byzantine cruciform rhythm, with a walnut iconostasis, houses two enormous icons of the archangels. A short distance outside the settlement lie the *churches of Agios Andronikos and Agia Marina*. Agios Andronikos church is very small and built with carved limestone rocks in a cruciform Byzantine style. The 15th century church of Agia Marina is arched and built with carved limestone.

Avgorou, 19 km north-west of Agia Napa, is a predominantly agricultural village. Its medieval and contemporary churches and monasteries are very interesting. Near the centre of the village stands the large church of *Agioi Petros and Pavlos* with an impressive carved iconostasis. A *Heroes Monument* has been erected by the community next to the church. The small, domed church of Agios Georgios in the centre of the village is peculiar in that it has a raised narthex. To the west of the village the visitor encounters the domed and cruciform *church of Agios Georgios "Teratsiotis"*, a 16th century building. To the north of the village, next to the old Nicosia-Famagusta road, the visitor comes across the *monastery of Agios Kendeas*. This monastery is built upon a small hillock overlooking the road. Most probably the domed church was built sometime during the 15th or 16th century.

Top: Cucumber glasshouse
Centre: Agios Andronikos, Frenaros
Bottom: White daisies in the fields

Text by Christina G. Karouzis

Photos from the archives of SELAS LTD

Published by the Center of Studies, Research & Publications SELAS LTD
P.O.Box 28619, 2081 Nicosia, Cyprus
www.selas.com.cy, e-mail: selas@spidernet.com.cy